G000276303

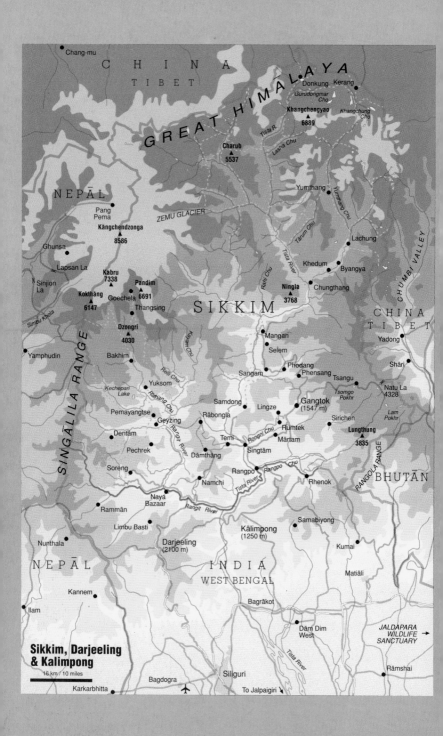

Sikkim, Darjeeling & Kalimpong

16 km / 10 miles

T_ashi Delek!_

Imagine that a friend has invited you to Sikkim, a tiny eastern Himalayan kingdom that made news in the 1960s when a young American woman wed into its royal family. That is probably all you know about it. But you trust your friend's judgment; she has lived and travelled extensively in the Himalaya for the last nine years and is herself married to a Sikkimese. Her name is Wendy Brewer Lama. She would accompany you on your travels if she could — besides being a writer and editor, she is a travel guide — ushering you into Sikkimese homes and leading you across high glacial passes.

Instead, Wendy has written her recommendations down in the form of this book. Your personalised journey begins in Gangtok, capital of Sikkim. Form there you can choose among various day excursions to Sikkim's treasure houses of art and folklore, its Tibetan Buddhist monasteries, stopping in picturesque villages along the way.

Sacrificing nothing to comfort, Wendy then takes you west to the sacred jewel of Sikkim, Pemayangstee Monastery, and to a pilgrimage lake. The pace is deliberately leisurely, for to hurry is to miss the essence of a place that has never known plastic-wrapper tourism. As extensive as are Sikkim's roads, you see the real beauty only if you get out and walk. Wendy suggests several day hikes and longer treks through magnificent forests with close-up mountain views.

Wendy's itineraries also take you to Darjeeling and Kalimpong where you find a wealth of history and adventure, and some less-touristy spots that you might otherwise have missed.

"Unspoilt" and "undiscovered" are too cliche for this part of the world. Here is a land of virgin forests and idyllic botanical conditions, of serene holy retreats and of a culture struggling to survive... where travelling is truly a privilege.

Tashi Delek! Welcome!

Insight Pocket Guide:

SIKKIM

First Edition

© 1993 APA Publications (HK) Ltd.

All Rights Reserved

Printed in Singapore by

Höfer Press (Pte) Ltd

Fax: 65-861 6438

No part of this book
may be reproduced, stored in a
retrieval system or transmitted
in any form or means electronic,
mechanical, photocopying,
recording or otherwise,
without prior written permission
of *Apa Publications*.
Brief text quotations with use of
photographs are exempted for
book review purposes only.

SIKKIM
DARJEELING & KALIMPONG

Written by **Wendy Brewer Lama**

Directed by **Hans Höfer**

Design Concept by **V. Barl**

Art Direction by **Patrick E. K. Wong**

Photography by **Sujoy Das, Wendy Brewer Lama,**
Gary McCue, Arthur Pazo and others

Edited by **Lisa Choegyal**

INSIGHT
pocket
GUIDES

Contents

Dear Reader

Unlike many would-be travellers who lust for accounts of far-off lands and dream of visiting them, it was not until after I had roamed far and wide throughout the Himalaya that I recalled my first impression of Sikkim. The *Los Angeles Times* and television talk shows carried news of Hope Cooke marrying the future King of Sikkim, a country unveiled for the first and for many the last time to viewers across the world. In my wildest dreams, I never imagined becoming a second American emissary to this stunning land and its endearing people, as I have through marriage to my Sikkimese husband.

Having lived for seven years in Nepal, it was surprisingly easy to enter my in-law's household and feel at home as an adopted native. Guests at our traditional wedding asked me to pass on their greetings to their *Gyalmo* (Queen), Hope Cooke, never imagining that her home in New York is a long 5,000 km (3,000 miles) away from mine in California.

During our numerous family visits, we have not only toured much of the countryside and trekked high into the Himalaya, but have participated in family rituals and religious festivals unique to the Sikkimese Bhutias, yet strongly reminiscent of the Tibetan traditions from whence they came.

As a tourism planner and travel writer – and an avid tourist myself – what impresses me most about Sikkim is its integrity, based largely on its allegiance to Buddhism. There are few places on earth where Mahayana Buddhism is so pervasive and overt. This ancient philosophy influences every layman and woman's behaviour and even government buildings are sculpted into monastic architectural masterpieces.

Physically, Sikkim is almost a single south-facing drainage scooped out of the east-west running Himalaya. In its tiny circumference is a miraculous variety of plants and animals ranging from tropical to alpine with all shades in between.

Travel in Sikkim is an enigma; relentlessly steep hills and knife-edge valleys stand between a developed capital and a largely agricultural landscape, yet villages are lit by electricity and running water is available virtually to all. Schools and rural development schemes have lifted farmers above subsistence level and nowadays most young people speak English and compete for estimable jobs. Well paved roads bridge the distances where telephones have not yet reached.

The traveller can thus roam deep into the hills in unexpected comfort, staying in pleasant government guest houses and hotels of Western standards. Trails are virtually free of litter and sanitation is noticeably good.

But most remarkable are the people, with values untarnished by commercialisation and, although perhaps with a slight naivety in approaching tourists, without dual motives or surreptitious ambitions. It is natural for visitors to breathe a sigh of relief when entering Sikkim's snow-lion guarded gates, knowing that barriers can be relaxed and the struggles of travel through other parts of India are behind them.

Darjeeling is just a valley away and complements Sikkim's indigenous appeal with more traditional tourist attractions, and some of the most well touted tea in the world. Today the hillstation preserves many of the British Raj's residual charms, with stately gardens, toy train rides, proper English guest houses and even some trekking to the border hills.

Once a rival in Tibet trade, Kalimpong still demands attention separate from Sikkim and Darjeeling. The smallest yet once most cosmopolitan of the three crest-top towns is blessed with an unhurried atmosphere, perfect climate and Victorian gardens bursting with colour.

This book encapsulates the essence of each place as I have come to know it. It's up to you to paint your own experience. Breathe in the fresh morning air alive with *lamas'* chanting, and explore native forests like few remaining on earth. I hope that you will find a purity of mind and heart as I have discovered in this hidden corner of the Himalaya.

Wendy Brewer Lama.

A Natural Amphitheatre

Though its political influence once extended further east and west, Sikkim's present day boundaries follow logical natural barriers. Mountains reaching up to 7,000 - 8,000 m (23,000 - 26,000 ft) wrap around it on three sides, and the mighty Rangit and Tista Rivers with their tributaries define it to the south.

The Himalayan ramparts are what brought Sikkim under the wings of India as the 22nd state in 1975, while it was Darjeeling's climate and the strategic trade value of Kalimpong that made India, and others, covet them. The three domains combine to form a tiny political thumb protruding north from the arm that draws Assam and other northeastern states into India.

Sandwiched between Nepal on the west and Bhutan on the east, Sikkim's tiny area of about 65 by 113 km (40 by 70 miles), or 7,300 sq km (2,800 sq miles), gets easily lost on South Asia maps. Reaching from a low of 250 m (800 ft) above sea level up to the permanently frozen 8,586 m (28,169 ft) summit of **Kangchendzonga,** third highest mountain in the world, Sikkim nurtures

ecosystems of nearly every elevational strata. Its neighbour and ancestor Tibet abuts to the north and east, while India's own West Bengal state, with the hilltop communities of Darjeeling (2,134 m, 7,002 ft) and Kalimpong (1,250 m, 4,101 ft) straddle the Tista River to the south. Zeroing in close to 28 degrees north latitude and 88 degrees east longitude, its position is on par with Orlando, Florida and lies just south of Kuwait.

Resting in the lap of these largely impenetrable walls, Sikkim is in essence a giant natural amphitheatre emptying

Boys painting bamboo

The Rangit Valley

into the Bay of Bengal. A simple bamboo fan illustrates the drainage pattern, with each slender rib a crease – some as deep as 1,500 m (5,000 ft) – between ridges. The north-south oriented Rangit and Tista Rivers, fed by glacial lakes and the Lachung and Lachen Chu tributaries, create the two main watersheds, with a series of legends to explain their origins. As the story goes, a bird leading the headwaters of the Rangit and a serpent laying a track for the Tista decided to race to a meeting point. But along the way, the bird felt hungry and darted back and forth in search of food, while the serpent meandered only slightly, thus setting the characteristic course of each river.

Valley of Rice

Sikkim's bowl-shape is due to its geologic structure. Some 40 million years ago, there were intense pressures rearranging the earth's crust as the subcontinent of India pushed north into the shore of the Asian land mass, forming the Himalaya. At the time, the area which is now Sikkim may have been more consistently elevated. But because the rocks of the northern, western and eastern regions were hard gneisses, and those of the central and southern regions were soft, easily eroded slates and schists, the rims stood fast while the core was whittled down to an inhabitable and barely-farmable landscape. Nonetheless, relative to Tibet's high barren plateau, Sikkim's well-watered conditions rendered rice cultivation possible, and thus it is known among cousins to the north as *Denzong* or "Valley of Rice."

The Tista funnels the full brunt of a lusty monsoon into Sikkim and flushes the catchment with new life every June through August. Gangtok and Darjeeling record an average annual rainfall of around 325 cm (128 ins), one of the highest in the Himalaya, yet by the

Kangchendzonga, guardian deity

time the clouds reach the far north only 60 cm (24 ins) can be squeezed out. Somewhat sheltered, Kalimpong receives about 220 cm (87 ins) yearly. Temperatures likewise vary with elevation; narrow valley bottoms heat up to 35°C (95°F) during late spring while mid-elevation climes stay generally between 7°C and 25°C (45°F and 77°F). Above 3,000 m (10,000 ft), it often freezes during winter and warms to a year-round maximum of 15°C (60°F).

Orchids, Rhododendrons and Pandas

Sir J.D. Hooker, the 19th-century Himalayan botanist, catalogued some 2,920 plant species during his extensive field studies throughout Sikkim, Darjeeling and Kalimpong beginning in 1848. The eastern Himalaya is now thought to harbour an estimated 4,000 plant species. Following Hooker's classification of the area's vegetation by elevation, a tropical belt, extending up to 1,500 m (5,000 ft) features figs, bamboo, plantains, tree ferns, orchids, ferns, screw pines and numerous tree species including the hefty sal (*Shorea robusta*) with plate-size leaves, and the lanky kapok or silk cotton tree (*Bombax ceiba*) whose white trunks tower above a green canopy. Sal, a hard wood excellent for carpentry, once covered the

lower hills of Sikkim and West Bengal, but has been replaced with cultivation. Newly planted groves can be seen from the roadside approaching Rangpo along the lower Tista River.

High into temperate forests, oaks give way to laurels, chestnuts, maples, birch, magnolias, cherries and rhododendrons, with yew, cedars, larches, fir and junipers at the upper edges. Some 200 species of ferns and various mosses,

The classic cymbidium

vines and lichens form a thick undergrowth. The Bhutia and Lepcha peoples have an impressive command of plants, using them for medicine, food, fibre, construction, and decoration.

The cold and dryness of the approaching Tibetan plateau impose a tree line at around 4,000 m (13,000 ft). Vegetation shrinks to ground-hugging cushiony shrubs that retain maximum moisture. Miniature rhododendron leaves give off a strong scent and are collected for burning as incense in Buddhist monasteries. Yaks graze on alpine meadows, and above 4,800 m (15,700 ft) all turns white but for patches of dirt scoured lifeless atop wind-blasted passes. Glaciers stretch downward another 1,000 m (3,300 ft) evidently lower in earlier times judging by round-bottom valleys, abandoned moraines and alpine bathtub lakes.

Sikkim is world renowned for its orchids with 600 to 1,000

One of the 600 to 1000 orchid species

species in and around Sikkim, Kalimpong and Darjeeling at elevations from 300 m to 4,000 m (1,000 ft-13,000 ft). The well-guided visitor might encounter samples of as many as 150 to 200 species. The best time to see orchids in bloom at lower and mid-elevations is from the second week of April to the first week of May, extending later into May and June at higher reaches. The Orchid Sanctuary in Gangtok displays over 200 species. A walk-through orchid sanctuary is being developed in the Kalimpong area.

Rhododendrons are another of the most celebrated of this amazing *pot pourri* of flora. Their variety, abundance and splendour are a sheer delight to behold. During April-May, yellow and lavender shaded hillsides stretch as far as the eye can see, and canopies of rose, crimson and ivory crown the misty forests. Some 40 species have been identified in Sikkim and in the hills surrounding Kalimpong and Darjeeling. Interest in Himalayan rhododendrons began with the discovery in 1796 of the *Rhododendron arboreum*, the most widely dispersed variety with colours ranging from white to blood red. Most rhododendrons grow between elevations 2,500 m and 4,500 m (8,200 ft and 15,000 ft), but the *Rhododendron dalhousie* with large bell-like, fragrant flowers and a deadly nectar, comes in below 2,000 m (6,500 ft). The Sikkim Nature Conservation Foundation protects some of the endangered species of rhododendrons and other plants in their natural habitats. Members Sonam Lachungpa and K.C. Pradhan have produced a collector's item book titled *Sikkim-Himalayan Rhododendrons* with 49 hand painted plates of the blossoms and leaves.

The eastern Himalaya's prolific gardenscape supports a multitude of wildlife as well. Situated at the interface of two major zoological regions, the Oriental and Palaearctic, faunal representatives of both zones account for the great diversity. Birds and butterflies species number into the 600s, and moths may score as high as 2,000. The more common birds seen are kingfishers, woodpeckers, cuckoos, sunbirds, laughing-thrushes, babblers, bulbuls, finches, eagles, hawks, owls, pigeons, doves and pheasant of which the *kalij* is evident. Sikkim is said to contain more kinds of birds than any similar sized area in the world. Dr. Salim Ali gives a detailed account in his book *The Birds of Sikkim*.

Mammals who once found refuge in the area's extensive forests have been pushed to higher ground by

A wild orchid sanctuary

Yaks, ideal highland beasts of burden

widespread cultivation. Those of the tropical realm include the barking deer – more often picked out by its dog-like call than seen – jungle cats and mongoose. Residents of the temperate zone are the common langur monkey, with a silver coat and long dark tail, the leopard cat, and jackal, despised by poultry farmers. Less common are the musk deer, Himalayan black bear, goral, serow, *tahr* and red panda, the state animal of Sikkim but unfortunately endangered by a dwindling population. Alpine mammals recorded are the snow leopard, the wild ass, marmots and *bharal* (blue sheep). Domestic yaks also inhabit the highlands, valued for their dairy products, wool, meat and their ability to cross snow-bound passes.

Five refuges have been designated in Sikkim to help protect the native wildlife. Only two are open to foreign tourists: **Fambong Lho Wildlife Sanctuary**, located 20 km (12 miles) west of Gangtok, harbours cats, ungulates and other animals of the lower and middle elevations. The **Maenam Wildlife Sanctuary**, east of Tashiding Monastery, supports similar fauna within it 8,600 acres (3,500 hectares). Entrance to either requires permission from the Chief Wildlife Warden (Forest Secretariat, Gangtok). Three others are located within restricted regions. **Kangchendzonga National Park**, established in 1977 covers an 850 sq km (328 sq mile) high altitude area north of Mount Pandim. It takes in the Nepal-Sikkim border range featuring Tent Peak, Nepal Peak as well as peaks Siniolchu, Kabur North and South, Kangchendzonga and the Zemu glacier within Sikkim. **Shingba Rhododendron Sanctuary** near Yumthang is also in North Sikkim and **Kyongnosia Alpine Sanctuary** lies east of Gangtok near Tsangu Lake. The Deer Park in Gangtok contains a few varieties of deer and at times the red panda.

Kalimpong has turned its mild climate to advantage in a well developed horticulture industry, exporting both cut and potted flowers to India and abroad. Commercial nurseries (some open for tours on appointment) specialise in orchids, cacti, cymbidium, anthoriums, amaryllis, roses, dahlias and gladioli. The Lloyd Botanic Garden in Darjeeling nurtures Himalayan and alpine plants in a spacious setting just minutes from the city bazaar. Some 50 types of wild mammals and birds of the Himalaya and Central Asia are kept at the nearby zoo, including a number of rare species.

Lepcha "Woodmen"

There is little more than conjecture available to piece together the early history of Sikkim, which up until the last century included lands now occupied by Darjeeling and Kalimpong. The Lepchas, or

Himalayan Barred Owl

Rong as they call themselves, were the first known settlers and are thought to be of Indo-Chinese stock originally from Nagaland. Why and when they came remains a mystery, for they had no written language until the early 18th century when Sikkim's third Chogyal (the religious and secular king) of Tibetan lineage devised a Lepcha script to speed the introduction of Tibetan Buddhism.

Thus the dawn of civilisation in Sikkim remains shrouded in legend. The Lepchas' Creation Myth tells that Itbu-mu, the Great Mother Creator, and her male and female creations once resided in the land of the gods until the males and females took to co-habiting. Having bred demon offspring, all were relegated to earth.

The British (Risley's *Gazetteer of Sikhim* (sic), circa 1894) later described the Lepchas as "... above all things woodmen of the woods, knowing the ways of the birds and beasts, and possessing an extensive zoological and biological nomenclature of their own." During his 19th century wanderings, Sir Joseph Hooker, the British botanist, conferred that the Lepchas were indeed born naturalists and invaluable as companions: "A more interesting and attractive companion than the Lepcha I never lived with; cheerful, kind, and patient with a master to whom he is attached, rude but not savage, ignorant and yet intelligent; with a simple resource of a plain knife he makes his house and furnishes yours with a speed, alacrity and ingenuity that wile away that well-known long hour, when the weary pilgrim frets for his couch."

The Lepchas were content hunting and living off this land of abundance. Their numbers were small – in 1840, they numbered only 3,000 – and their nomadic lifestyle precluded any permanent settlements. Their religion, contrary to a later Christian interpretation as the worship of demons, propitiated the "evil spirits who dwell in every rock, grove or mountain, are constantly at mischief, and to them we must pray for they hurt us."

Bhutias "Lords of Sikkim"

So in balance with their world were the Lepchas that when a contingent of 17 Tibetans accompanying Khye-Bumsa ("the superior of 10,000 heroes") arrived in Gangtok in the 13th century, the venerable Lepcha leader Thekong Tek welcomed and blessed them, sensing no threat from his fabled warring neighbours. Thekong Tek foretold that Bumsa's descendants, of east Tibet's royal Namgyal lineage, would become lords of Sikkim and that the Lepcha would serve as common-people.

Monastery window with cremation pellets

Bumsa had earned his title of greatness while on pilgrimage from his home in Kham, east Tibet to Sakya, west of Lhasa, where a monastery was being built to serve the Sakyapas, the reigning sect of Tibetan Buddhism at that time. The seven story *lhakhang*'s (temple's) main strength was to come from four immense wooden pillars, which several thousand men had tried and failed to raise. The visiting pilgrim succeeded in erecting the supports, for which he was named Khye-Bumsa and was given the local heirarch's daughter in marriage. With time, proven childless, he was advised by *lamas* to travel south and pay homage to the Lepchas for which he would be blessed with three sons.

Having set in motion a lingering brotherhood with the Lepcha leader which was later to be sworn in blood, Bumsa returned to Tibet where his wife bore three sons. Bumsa's middle son, Miponrab ("Leader of Men") fathered four boys who would become the patriarchs of Sikkim's four major Bhutia (from *Bhote* or People of Tibet) families, carrying the Namgyal line through twelve generations to the present day. Tibetans had long considered *Denzong* (their name for Sikkim) and the *Denzongpas* ("People of *Denzong*" as they are known to this day) as an extension of the rich Chumbi Valley of south-central Tibet, though the snowbound passes of Natu La and Jelep La stood fast between. The Lepchas welcomed their Tibetan brother Guru Tashi, youngest of Bumsa's grandsons, when he settled in Sikkim and upon the death of Thekong Tek turned to him for leadership. Guru Tashi's great-grandson Phuntsog Namgyal, became the first Chogyal of Sikkim.

"King of Religion"

The story of how Phuntsog Namgyal became Chogyal again involved a directive from Tibetan *lamas*. Fleeing the rise of the reform-minded, dominant Gelugpa sect in Tibet, three "Learned Ones" of the traditional Nyingmapa school met near Yuksom in west Sikkim to select a lay ruler for "The Valley of Rice." Among

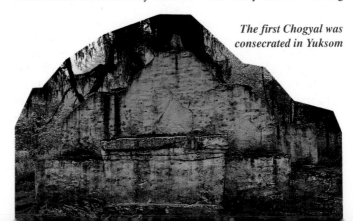

The first Chogyal was consecrated in Yuksom

them was Lhatsun Chempo, honoured as the founder of the Nyingmapa sect in Sikkim. Sacred texts had revealed that the ruler designate would be a man named Phuntsog of Gangtok, so the *lamas* sent an envoy in search of him. The party returned with Phuntsog Namgyal, and in 1642 he was crowned with all due rites as Sikkim's first Chogyal, "King Who Rules With Righteousness" or literally "King of Religion".

Phuntsog was promptly recognised as a holy leader by Tibet's Dalai Lama, and proceeded to set up a centralised administration whose capital was to be Yuksom. He divided the kingdom into 12 *dzongs* (forts or districts), each under a Lepcha governor, and appointed 12 Bhutia ministers. At that time, his realm was much larger than today's, stretching south onto the plains of northern Bihar and what is now Bangla-

Denzong, Valley of Rice

desh, west to the Arun River in today's Nepal, and east to the Taigon pass, encompassing Kalimpong and parts of present day Bhutan. Owing allegiance to the ultimate religious authority (as well as their blood ties) in Tibet, Sikkim continued to look north for religious and political advice. The bonds were cemented by the first and subsequent Chogyals taking a Tibetan wife.

By this time, Sikkim was as much the domicile of the Bhutias as the Lepchas. The Limbus, called *Tsong* by the Tibetans, were also among the early settlers although little is mentioned of them in historical texts. Believed to have originated in Tibet's Tsangpo Valley and settled in east Nepal, it was they who christened their adopted homeland *Sukhim* (later evolved to Sikkim) or "Happy Home". The Tibetan term *"Lho-Mon-Tsong-sum"* describes the Limbus alongside the Bhutias and Lepchas as the indigenous people of Sikkim.

British Raj

Battered by continued invasions from both east and west, Sikkim often sought the protection of Tibet. Lhasa helped restore the new capital at Rabdentse when it was captured and held for eight years by Bhutan. The third Chogyal Chador Namgyal again drove out the Bhutanese but lost Kalimpong in the shuffle. Nepal succeeded in occupying Sikkim east to the Tista River, taking Darjeeling and the better part of the kingdom. Not until the treaty of Titalia in 1817 was a substantial part of the territory restored to Sikkim with assistance from (and sizable chunks retained by) the British, but not without heavy strings attached.

The British Raj was now in its heyday, and to keep relations on

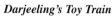
Darjeeling's Toy Train

an even keel, Sikkim gave the East India Company a deed for Darjeeling to be used as a sanatorium. The British found the fresh climate suitable for recovery and escape from the overbearing lowland heat. Soon Darjeeling supplanted India's older hillstations' fading charms. The construction of Hill Cart Road in 1839, linking the hilltop with the plains, and in 1882 completion of the Northern Bengal State Railway between Calcutta and Darjeeling, more fondly known as the "Toy Train", set in motion the development of Darjeeling not only as a tea centre but eventually as a trans-Himalayan trade depot and a chic rendezvous spot for Raj socialites.

With the introduction of tea gardens in the 1850s, the face of Darjeeling was changed forever. Slopes once thick with forests were now stripped for tea plantations and residences for thousands of imported Nepalese tea labourers. The native peoples, primarily Lepchas, began to feel squeezed and many migrated to Nepal. By 1872 the hill district boasted a residency of 47,000, with the Lepchas amounting to no more than 3,900.

Within ten years, 39 estates had been planted. Tea bushes imported from China produced an aromatic black tea that quickly gained international favour. Soon British tea planters had attained a degree of prestige and wealth that demanded gala weekend parties attended by the cream of Calcutta. The pretentious Planters' Club served imported ports, hogshead beer, plum puddings and reserved its dining rooms only for male guests.

By the early 1900s, Darjeeling was in a social swirl, fostering many a summer romance in its acquired Victorian setting. Inns such as the Windamere Hotel hosted the likes of the King and Queen of Belgium and the Begum Aga Khan and witnessed 40 years later the flirtations of Sikkim's Chogyal Palden Thondup and the young Hope Cooke. Remnants of that golden age survive today in the Windamere's cosy charms enhanced by photographs and memorabilia adorning its velvet-furbished sitting rooms.

Tea and Trade Troubles

Relations between Sikkim and Darjeeling soured over the extradition of slaves and criminals, followed by the detention of Campbell and Hooker during an 1859 unauthorised trip to Sikkim. The British Indian Government forced a treaty on Sikkim in 1861 annexing the whole of Darjeeling, obtaining agreement to build a

Sikkim's last reigning
Chogyal and Gyalmo

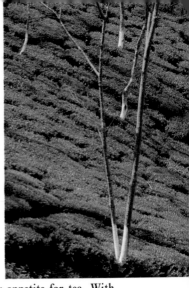

trade road through Sikkim to Tibet, and establishing a military presence to regulate Sikkim's foreign relations. At the same time India claimed the Duars, the only flat-lands of Bhutan, at the close of the 1865 war and acquired Kalimpong along with valuable tea lands.

From the Gurkha War of 1814, the British had seen advantage in extending goodwill to Sikkim, their objective to at-tain passage to trade relations with Tibet and eventually China. Exchanges between Sikkim and Tibet over the Jelep La, east of Gangtok, had been going on for centuries. Now Darjeeling wanted a piece of the pie, particularly to supply the Tibetans' healthy appetite for tea. With agreement apparently sewn up with Sikkim, only Peking's watchful eye over Tibet and Sikkim's foreign involvement posed a potential roadblock. For a time, China gave cautious agreement and trade prospered. But obstacles, namely the Tibetans' hesitancy to allow foreigners access, entered the picture. When efforts to communicate by personal letter from India's Viceroy Curzon to the Dalai Lama failed, the British made preparations – by building a road from Gangtok to Chumbi – to send a mission to Tibet with armed escort under Colonel Francis Younghusband.

Sikkim's Chogyal attempted to intervene, warning Tibet of the British military strength, but in vain and the Tibetans suffered a disheartening military defeat by Younghusband at Gyantse in 1904. Eventually, the Tibetans came to terms with the British at the Lhasa Convention, and the long sought-after trade permission was given. In the end, Sikkim gained little from the deal with the high costs of road maintenance and a loss of its own trade revenue; but mostly, by India's assertion of suzerainty in Sikkim's affairs.

British India was to continue making inroads into Sikkim. The forthright Political Officer Claude White periodically banished the Chogyal to outposts, and as part of a scheme to inject a majority voice against Tibetan influence White invited thousands of Nepalese to settle in Sikkim under the guise of broadening the public works tax base. By the turn of the 20th century, the Nepalese had become a clear majority, outnumbering the Lho-Mon-Tsong-sum in both numbers and political voice.

A similar alignment of population was occurring in Darjeeling and Kalimpong. Tibetans, Marwaris (Indian businessmen), Nepalis and Bengalis read the stars of opportunity in these thriving hill economies and their varied presence painted a colourful cosmopoli-tan scene. Darjeeling prospered in tea, tourism and trade; Kalimpong followed suit of Sikkim and grew as a major trade post

with Tibet, supervised largely by the Marwaris.

To step into either town in the early 1900s would have offered quite a sight. Mountaineering reconnaissance teams approaching Everest through Darjeeling added intrigue and heroics to club parties. Tibetan wool loaded on mule caravans wound its way from Kalimpong to the Calcutta docks and on to carpet and blanket factories in America and Europe. Tibetan aristocracy accompanying children to the hillstations' schools gathered at Kalimpong's Himalaya Hotel to play pontoon and rummy with the Europeans, and to sing and dance with the Sikkimese. Scottish Christian missionaries built steepled churches and found a ready ear in the Lepchas.

Though the Sikkimese Buddhists were relatively accommodating to their Nepalese Hindu newcomers, the Chogyals staunchly forbade the intrusion of Christianity into the kingdom. But not so with secular evolution. Beginning with Sidkeong Tulku, educated at Oxford and invested as tenth Chogyal in 1914, and more emphatically with his successor Tashi Namgyal, Sikkim was to see many administrative, political and judicial reforms in this century. Far reaching development projects, funded generously by India, introduced a much improved standard of living to Sikkim's rural populations, and a multi-party system eventually ushered in an elected council of ministers. Foreign Buddhist scholars and naturalists were invited to study here, as the world gradually took note of this tiny kingdom so rich in natural resources and religious heritage.

The American Queen

But what finally grabbed the international media was the wedding of Crown Prince Palden Thondup to American Hope Cooke in 1963. The Prince had been married to a Tibetan, Sangey Deki, who bore him three children but her untimely death left him grieved and the country without a Gyalmo. After the prescribed mourning period for the 1962 death of his father Sir Tashi, the Coronation of

Palden Thondup took place with much pomp and ceremony on April 4, 1965. Draped in silk brocade, the royal entourage approached the Tsuklakhang (Royal Chapel) at the auspicious hour of 9.30 a.m. Ambassadors, special representatives of India, Bhutan and Nepal, foreign dignitaries, journalists and photographers crowded into the gilded quarters. Rituals were performed to ward off evil spirits and to usher in a tranquil atmosphere where good powers would reign. Royal vestments and auspicious objects symbolising longevity, prosperity and honouring the eternal Doctrine of Buddha were offered. Finally the guests and public gave the newlyweds *katas*, white silk ceremonial scarves and gifts carried from afar. and all joined in a sumptuous Sikkimese feast.

But the sugar-coated marriage, and the kingdom itself, was to last little more than ten years. Despite efforts to introduce democratic reforms, the Chogyal and Gyalmo became targets of unrest, prodded by a Nepalese majority demanding greater voice, and the palace rule crumbled. An independent India exerted itself, building up a militia force ready to counter an imagined Chinese assault. On May 16, 1975 Sikkim became a state of India and the heart-broken Chogyal was resigned to serve only as a figurehead. Hope Cooke moved with the children back to New York and in December 1981 Palden Thondup Namgyal died of cancer in America.

Sikkim Today

Today Sikkim is administered by a strong Chief Minister N.B. Bhandari, who commands support by his ability to address the

Butter sculpture, water, light – offerings to the gods

needs of a diverse people. The Nepalese constitute 75 percent of the population, the Lho-Mon-Tsong-sum – the Lepchas, Bhutias and Limbus – together make up a shrinking minority. There is a smattering of Indians, even some Moslems and a small population of Tibetan refugees who settled here after fleeing Tibet in the 1960s.

As recorded in Arthur Foning's personalised book *Lepcha, My Vanishing Tribe*, the Lepcha population of Sikkim, Darjeeling and Kalimpong is continuing to shrink as more and more intermarry with Bhutias and Nepalis. Though some have clung to their own religion and customs, others are happy to be Christians. In Sikkim, the remaining Lepchas are concentrated in the northern valleys and though still mainly occupied by farming are also active in business and politics. Lepcha language has largely given way to Nepali, now prevalent throughout Sikkim.

The Bhutias have carried on within their Tibetan tradition. The women wear a long wrap-around dress called a *kho* tied in the back over a silk blouse (*honju*). Married women add a striped apron called a *pangden*. Most Bhutia men only sport their native dress, also called a *kho*, on special occasions; dark wool for official functions and brocade silk for weddings. With a high neck-cut distinct from the Tibetan and Bhutanese styles, the knee length robe is bunched in the back and tied with a silk sash.

Whereas it was once common for a Bhutia woman (like her Tibetan ancestors) to marry several brothers, monogamous marriages are by far the modern mode. Depending on her family's preference, she will often select her own husband or be consulted in her parents' choice. Women are educated and hold prestigious positions in government and industry.

At one time, the second son of every Bhutia family entered a monastery as a monk, but nowadays interest in secular education and professions are stronger pulls. Those who join the monastery do so at the age of six or seven and live separate from their parents, diligently studying the sacred scripts and rituals which will qualify them for *lama*-hood. The community *lama* plays an important role in social as well as religious functions, blessing marriages, conducting funerals and staging ceremonies to break a curse or an individual's bad luck.

The Nepalese of Sikkim are now firmly woven into the fabric and hold administrative posts as well as run private businesses. Representing a cross-section of Nepal's multitude of ethnic groups, they figure as Hindu Indo-Aryans such as Brahmans and Chhetris, Buddhists of Tibetan stock such as Sherpas, Tamangs and Gurungs, a mix of two heritages such as in the Newars, as well as Rais and Limbus with their own animist religion. Those of Aryan features are easily discernible by their long noses, wider eyes and lanky bodies in contrast to the Bhutias, Lepchas and Nepalese of Mongoloid stock with round faces, almond eyes and stockier frames.

HISTORY

Pre-History: The first known people to settle in Sikkim, the Lepchas, are thought to have found their way through what is now Assam from Nagaland. For centuries they live as hunters and gatherers.

A.D. 600: The great King Songtsengampo of Tibet, forefather of Khye-Bumsa, Patriarch of the royal Namgyal family in Sikkim, is born and propagates Buddhism in Tibet.

1300s: Lepcha leader Thekong Tek welcomes Bumsa and his entourage of 17 Tibetans to Sikkim, paving the way for a peaceful introduction of the Bhutia lords and lineage.

1642: Phuntsog Namgyal, descendant of Bumsa, is crowned as Sikkim's first Chogyal in Yuksom. He sets up a centralised administration over lands reaching east and west of present day Sikkim.

1700s: Sikkim is frequently attacked by Bhutanese and Nepalese forces. The new capital, Rabdentse, is occupied and Tibet intervenes on behalf of Sikkim.

1817: The Treaty of Titalia between British India and Sikkim restores Nepalese-occupied territory to Sikkim, setting the stage for Sikkim's southern neighbour to involve itself in Sikkim's affairs.

1850-1900: Tea estates invade the Darjeeling slopes and Nepalese labourers follow. Darjeeling becomes the Raj's favourite hillstation and sanatorium, awhirl with richly-catered parties and royal romances.

1910-1940: Kalimpong vies with Darjeeling and Sikkim as a Tibetan trade post; highland wool travels to Western carpet factories and India's aromatic teas rival China's own.

1914: Sikkim's tenth Chogyal Sidkeong Tulku, Oxford educated, takes the throne and introduces political reforms. These are continued by his successor Sir Tashi Namgyal, who seeks vast improvements for his people and introduces an electoral government.

1950-1960s: An independent India's watchful eye on Tibet, and an equally distrustful China moving ever closer, squelch trans-Himalayan trade. Darjeeling invites foreign tourists, Kalimpong turns to horticulture and Sikkim benefits from generous development funding from India.

1963: Crown Prince Palden Thondup marries American debutante Hope Cooke in a spectacular ceremony, capturing the world's attention for the first but not the last time. They succeed to the throne in 1965, but neither their marriage nor kingdom survive a decade.

1973: Growing agitation against the monarchy, led by a Nepalese majority, leads to the administration's collapse and Indian troops step in, followed by political arm wrestling for power.

1975: Sikkim becomes India's 22nd state, and the Chogyal retires to an empty palace atop the hill.

1981: Palden Thondup dies, some of his children having joined Hope Cooke in America.

1988-1989: Violent unrest demanding an independent state for Darjeeling and Kalimpong shut down business; a Hill Council is set up with greater ties to the central government.

1990s: A relaxation of strife and new visa regulations open the doors to tourism in all three enclaves.

Your stay in Sikkim begins in Gangtok, then venture into the countryside to experience its natural wonders and splendid monasteries. Even to those unschooled in Tibetan Buddhism, these centres of spiritual learning are fascinating places to visit. In Rumtek, home of Sikkim's leading reincarnate Karmapa Rinpoche, with its priceless paintings and ornate gold-encrusted shrines, and in the famous Pemayangtse and Tashiding monasteries, are preserved ancient treasures and a continuity of tradition unspoiled by the ravages of religious invaders.

Day ①

Gangtok

View the city of Gangtok and Mount Kangchendzonga from the vantage of Enchey Monastery. Stroll in the Deer Park and visit the Research Institute of Tibetology, Do-Drul Chorten and the Orchid Sanctuary. Take a Tibetan lunch in town and spend the afternoon with artisans at the handicraft and handloom centre and explore Gangtok's bazaar.

The sun rises early in the eastern Himalaya, and Sikkimese hospitality greets it with a cup of tea in bed while dawn's rays ignite a snowy glow on **Kangchendzonga**, third highest mountain in the world. At this moment in monasteries throughout the land, *lamas* and monks make ritual offerings of incense, butter and water to the country's guardian god, Kangchendzonga. Every Sikkimese house is

oriented north to face the great protector and the year's grandest festival is staged in the deity's honour.

Kangchendzonga means "Repository of Five Treasures", alluding to a legendary storehouse of gold, silver, gems, grains and holy books stowed within the five summits. Though Kangchendzonga reigns with benevolence, his cohort Yabdu (Black Father Devil) demands blood sacrifice to appease his malignant disposition. To humour these powerful forces, mountaineering expeditions have been forbidden until recently and must not step on the sacred summit.

Gangtok, meaning "The Hill Made Flat", served as the royal and administrative seat of the Kingdom of Sikkim from 1894 to 1975 and now as the state capital it retains a royal character. The Chogyal's durbar (king's palace) crowns the ridge, naturally facing Kangchendzonga, and the yellow roof of the **Tsuklakhang** or Royal Chapel gleams from far across the valley.

Clinging to a forested hillside, Gangtok is Sikkim's largest city but even that modest accolade belies its small town charms. Narrow streets snake up steep forested inclines to a towering television antenna stationed opposite a Buddhist monastery, epitomising the

Tobacco leaves and dried fish in Lall Market

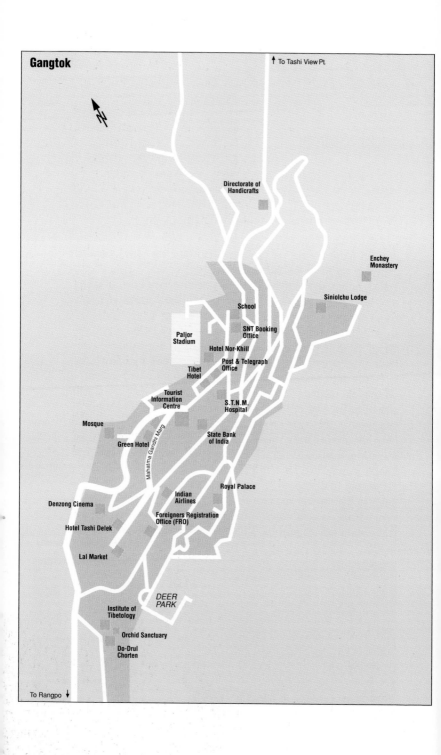

Gangtok

↑ To Tashi View Pt.

Directorate of
Handicrafts

Enchey
Monastery

Siniolchu Lodge

School

SNT Booking
Office

Paljor
Stadium

Hotel Nor-Khill

Post & Telegraph
Office

Tibet
Hotel

Tourist
Information
Centre

S.T.N.M.
Hospital

Mosque

State Bank
of India

Green Hotel

Mahatma Gandhi Marg

Royal Palace

Denzong Cinema

Indian
Airlines

Foreigners Registration
Office (FRO)

Hotel Tashi Delek

Lal Market

DEER
PARK

Institute of
Tibetology

Orchid Sanctuary

Do-Drul
Chorten

To Rangpo ↓

mingling of the secular and saintly worlds. The city's only straight, flat street is the three-block long commercial hub of **Mahatma Gandhi Marg**, dropping abruptly to the covered stall vegetable bazaar – the **Lall Bazaar**. With a population of 50,000 people – a tenth of the state's estimated half million – everyone knows each other and the visitor is quick to gain friendly recognition.

On this first morning in Gangtok, take a quick surveillance of the landscape from the ridgetop near **Enchey Monastery.** After breakfast in your hotel, grab a taxi and drive ten minutes out of the city centre, climbing past a stately Catholic church and into the cool forests that shade upper Gangtok. Just below the hillcrest, the road turns by the government-run **Siniolchu Lodge** named for one of Sikkim's peaks, and stops beneath the space-age television tower. Park here and walk a few minutes to Enchey Monastery.

Enchey originated as a hermitage and bears the fitting name "Place of Solitude". Built 150 years ago under the reign Chogyal Sidkeong Namgyal, this small *gompa* houses 90 monks of the Nyingmapa sect, beside Kargyudpa the primary sects of Tibetan Buddhism practised in Sikkim. Remember that out of respect for religious beliefs, you should circle any holy place in a clockwise direction and enter it with reverence in dress and behaviour.

Two large white conch shells used in ritual ceremony guard the monastery's large ornate doors. The conch is one of eight auspicious Buddhist symbols representing the awakening of one through the *dharma* (Buddhist tenets) to working for the benefit of others. Inside, dimly lit by butter lamps is a figure of Buddha, and painted frescoes line the walls. Images of benevolent deities contrast with the horrors of the protecting gods whose purpose is to drive away evil influences such as ignorance, lust and greed. Drums mounted at the ends of long cushioned seats are beaten by young monks to call attention to their prayers and meditation.

From outside the tiered red and white structure, with exaggerated window frames painted in typical trapezoidal *gompa* style, a staircase leads up to two small rooms, their doors painted with the frightening faces of wrathful deities, ringed by miniature skulls. The visitor is welcome to peek inside (this is one place where women are not allowed to enter) if the rooms are not in use, but often a private *puja* or ritual prayer ceremony is underway. An annual *chaam* dance ceremony is held at Enchey in winter.

It is a short drive to the **Royal Durbar** where every Chogyal between 1894 and 1975 lived and ruled. The palace is now closed to visitors. Nearby is the yellow-roofed Tsuklakhang where two important annual dance rituals are staged, Pang Lhabsol and

Enchey, Place of Solitude

Kagyat, honouring God Kangchendzonga and ushering in the Sikkimese New Year. The public is only allowed entrance at these festival times. Visitors are welcome however at **Tashiling**, the government secretariat located on the ridge shoulder, although the attractive exterior holds only the usual plain administrative offices.

At the **Deer Park** take a short walk in the shady forest. Deer and the red panda can be seen here, and a statue of Buddha. The Park is only open from 8-11 a.m. on weekdays (8 a.m.- 5 p.m. on Sundays and holidays) so plan an early arrival.

A few minutes' drive via the main highway drops you at the **Research Institute of Tibetology**, a museum of Buddhist scripts, ritual objects and art accessible to visitors and serious Tibetophiles

(open 10 a.m.- 4 p.m. daily except government holidays, closed during July, August and December. Tel: 2525). Among its rare collection of early artifacts is a series of silk embroidered *thangkas*, one of three sets of 18 made for the present Dalai Lama's enthronement and smuggled out of Tibet.

A short walk up the hill is rewarded with the massive gleaming white **Do-Drul Chorten**, one of the most important reliquary stupas in Sikkim. Also known as the Phurba Chorten, it contains *mandalas* of the Dorje Phurba sacred manuscripts and other powerful ritual objects. Surrounding the *chorten* are 108 prayer wheels. As devotees spin these always clockwise, they release the mantra *Om Mani Padme Hum* (Oh Blessed is the Jewel of the Lotus Blossom) which is written on papers rolled inside.

Study centres, an assembly hall and a small *gompa* share the hilltop with the large *chorten* alongside a smaller one built in 1962 in memory of Trulsi Rinpoche, head of the Ny-

Do-Drul reliquary chorten

ingmapa order who in 1945 built the Do-Drul Chorten.

Chortens like this one follow a customary design symbolising the elements; the solid square or rectangular base represents earth, above it a globe signifies water and on top a cone for fire. A crescent facing skyward indicates air and the top knob is ether. The cone is usually a series of thirteen tiers, often golden, which represent umbrellas, the symbol of royalty connoting protection but is also explained as the thirteen steps toward reaching *nirvana*.

On the walk back down the hill, you pass a large elongated rock known as "Stone Horse" or **Do-Ta-Bu**, as explained on a small plaque. Just beyond is the fenced **Orchid Sanctuary**. During spring (April-May) be sure to visit this garden harbouring some 200 varieties of orchids. Sikkim is blessed with hundreds of orchid species;

Selling pulses and spices

the *Dendrobium nobile* is the State Flower of Sikkim. An annual **International Flower Festival** held during spring displays a wealth of brilliant orchids, rhododendrons and other flowering plants in Gangtok's **White Hall**.

Return to Gangtok proper and enjoy lunch of a Sikkimese-Tibetan speciality known as *momos.* Many restaurants in town serve these small meat (pork or beef) stuffed dumplings steamed (or fried, known as *kothay*), customarily eaten with spicy chili sauce and a clear broth. The **Green Hotel** on Mahatma Gandhi (M.G.) Marg near the Tourist Information Centre is popular among locals and claim to serve between four and five thousand *momos* per day. The **Hotel Tibet**, just up from the Post Office, prepares *momos* as well as *shabalay* (a delicious fried meat pastry) amidst elegant Tibetan decor.

Burn off an over-indulgence of *momos* — the proper way to eat them — with a 15-20 minute walk uphill to the **Directorate of Handicrafts and Handloom**, also known as the Government Institute of Cottage Industries; or catch a taxi and either ask the driver to wait or walk back down. The centre trains and employs about 200 rural and tribal Sikkimese in traditional handicraft production, including handloom weaving, woodcarving, bamboo works, *thangka* painting, knitting, sewing and carpetweaving. All goods are on sale in the Sales Room, open 10 a.m.- 4 p.m. daily, including Sundays. Small foldable tables called *choktse*, decorated with hand-carved dragons, flowers and birds in natural wood or colourfully painted, as seen in every Sikkimese home and monastery, are sold at very reasonable prices (about US$40). Attractive block-printed or hand-painted stationery of a wood-crafted paper (much like rice paper) or on handsome re-cycled paper is available. Visitors are welcome to tour the workshops.

End the afternoon window shopping and people watching wandering through the main bazaar along **Mahatma Gandhi Marg**, named for India's great peace leader. Souvenir items include Tibetan Buddhist ritual objects such as the *dorje* (thunderbolt), *phurba* (dagger) and bell, necklaces and bracelets of silver, brass and chunky coral and amber, bags of

A hand-carved mani stone at Tashiding

all sorts and miscellaneous boxes, vases and bowls. Below M.G. Marg lies **Lall Market**, selling vegetable and commodities in open-air stalls. It is a fun place to browse, particularly on Sunday mornings when crowds of hill-farmers and herders gather with their home-grown produce at the weekly bazaar.

Walk back to your hotel for dinner, enjoying the sunset as it bathes Kangchendzonga in golden light while Gangtok and you both retire to a quiet evening.

Rumtek

The impressive Rumtek Monastery, a 45 minute drive from Gangtok, is the seat of Karmapa Rinpoche. Walk through the neighbouring Jawaharlal Nehru Botanical Gardens or down to the old monastery. After lunch return to Gangtok on a quiet country road.

Although Pemayangtse Monastery is the premier of Sikkim's holy sanctums, **Rumtek Monastery and the Dharma Chakra Centre**, is the newest and perhaps the most impressive in size and grandeur. It is located 24 km (15 miles) by road from Gangtok and warrants a leisurely visit taking in its splendorous architecture and reverent atmosphere. Bring a packed lunch to savour in this serene surrounding, or sample some Nepalese-style *dal bhaat takari* (rice with lentils and vegetables) or *thukpa* (Tibetan noodle soup) in one of the small hotel restaurants (you have to pre-order or be prepared to wait).

Rumtek is the seat of His Holiness Karmapa Rinpoche, head of the Karmapa sub-sect of Kargyudpa order of Tibetan Buddhism.

Rumtek, seat of the Kargyudpa order

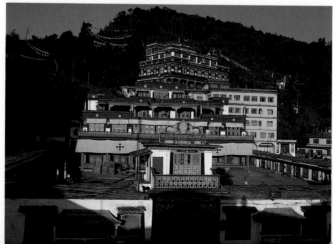

Like His Holiness the Dalai Lama, leader of the Gelugpa sect, the Karmapa Rinpoche (literally Precious One) is a reincarnate *lama* much revered by the Sikkimese people. Portraits of the 16th Karmapa, who passed away in 1981, are seen in every Kargyudpa monastery showing a kindly round face and ornate black hat which he holds on his head with one hand. The hat is said to have the power of flight and if not held down or kept tight in a special box will fly away.

A young monk spying on his peers

The origins of the Karmapa's distinctive black hat trace back to the first Karmapa who was born in Tibet in 1191. In a previous lifetime as a *lama*, he had completed a retreat of many years meditating in a cave whence 100,000 *dakhinis* (female spirits) came to congratulate him. Each made an offering of a hair from which the original black crown was woven. But the common man could not see the hat for it was invisible to all but those of elevated powers. Later, when the first Karmapa was visiting the king and queen of China, the queen offered to replace the hat with one that could be seen by all. Each of the sixteen Karmapas is portrayed wearing the magic black hat. It is said that people who look on the hat will not go to hell.

It was the ninth Karmapa who requested the fourth Sikkimese Chogyal to build a monastery in Sikkim, long considered an exceptionally holy place by Tibetan Buddhists. Early scripts had identified Sikkim, along with other protected and fertile valleys of the Himalaya, as sanctuaries of peace or *beyuls* where the Tibetan people could take refuge in times of strife or persecution.

Sikkim's first Karmapa *gompa* (monastery) was built at Ralong in 1730, and subsequently at Rumtek in 1740. The old Rumtek monastery was destroyed by earthquake but has now been restored and sits just below the new complex, built to house the 16th Karmapa when he fled from Tibet in the 1960s.

The new four-level *gompa* was designed as a replica of the Kargyudpas' head monastery at Tolung in Tibet. Its spacious interior is held up by robust red pillars, hung with long tubular silk banners. More than a hundred monks sit on the red and gold benches dur-

ing their morning and evening prayers. If you are spending the night at Rumtek, ask if you can attend a session. It is a sensational experience, one that touches every sense; a chorus of monks chant in deep non-melodic tones, occasionally beating drums and blowing horns, and butter lamps exude a golden light and a musty smell. Before leaving, you might want to leave a small donation at the altar or in an offering box to help support the monastery and to show your respect.

Upstairs from the main *gompa* are three levels containing separate *puja* rooms and on top the private quarters of His Holiness the Karmapa. Be sure to ask permission before entering any of these rooms, and of course to remove your shoes.

Surrounding the *gompa* is a **large courtyard,** the stage for Rumtek's annual ceremonial dance performances; Tse Chu *chaam* dances are usually held in June and the winter *chaams* just before Losar or Tibetan New Year in February.

The Karma Shri Nalanda Institute for Higher Buddhist Studies, constructed in 1984, stands directly behind the *gompa* and is itself a masterpiece of traditional Tibetan Buddhist architecture. Every colour of the rainbow, highlighted generously in gold, adorns the facade. A plaque inside lists those who donated to its construction.

Climb to the third floor and enter the main prayer hall; if the doorway is littered with shoes, prayers are in session and it would be better to come back later. The hall has exquisite wall and ceiling paintings, and altar figures of the 16th Karmapa, Sakyamuni Buddha and Manjushri. In contrast to other older monasteries, this room is large, well lit and still has a new gleam to the paint.

Rumtek's monks come from all over Sikkim, India, Nepal, Tibet and Bhutan. They complete a minimum nine year course of study at

Prayers inside the gompa

Rumtek's black hat dancers

the centre and can elect to spend another three years in isolated meditation in a small house above the monastery. They then graduate and are placed in any of several hundred Karma Kargyudpa centres around the world.

Exiting the Dharma Chakra Centre walk up the opposite flight of stairs to a room containing the **Reliquary Stupa of His Holiness the 16th Karmapa**. Be sure to seek permission to enter for herein lies a magnificent stupa (or *chorten*), plated in gold and bejewelled with turquoise and coral. Inside the stupa are sacred relics of bone and ash of the 16th Karmapa. Surrounding the central stupa are statues of each of the 16 Karmapas, centred around figures of Dorje Chhang, Marpa, the 11th century founder of the Kargyudpa sect, Tilopa and Naropa, his Indian teachers, and Milarepa, Marpa's much loved disciple. Milarepa, who is often shown holding his hand to his ear ever hearing the *dharma* in melody, is well known for having passed long retreats in a cave in central Tibet subsisting only on nettles until his body and hair turned green. Do not overlook the embroidered silk *thangka* of Karmapa in black headdress over the donation box opposite the entrance.

Since the passing of the 16th Karmapa, Sikkim has anxiously awaited the identification of the next incarnation. At a prescribed time and place, interpreted by auspicious signs and revelations obtained through the *lamas'* intense meditation, several young boys will be tested for distinguishing marks or behaviour and for their ability to identify their predecessor's personal objects. The chosen one will then be enthroned as the new Karmapa.

The **old Rumtek** *gompa* can be visited after lunch. A path leads down for about 10 minutes walk until the cedar forest clearing is in sight. Approach the monastery through a gate of laid tree limbs, often closed to keep the cows out. Notice several abandoned houses on your left built in the old Sikkimese style with crisscrossed wooden windows and an upper story of wood over a bottom floor of stone. A more serene setting could not be imagined. Overlooking a well-kept lawn posted with lanky prayer flags, monks sometimes gather here to practice their lessons, writing with a bamboo "pen" dipped in a watery ink on heavy rectangular slates. After each lesson, the slate is wiped clean.

Inside, the monastery is adorned with modest religious trappings compared to the new one. Upstairs is a small room with paintings of scripture scenes.

Departing from the old *gompa*, return along the same road. Instead of taking the short-cut path up to the lodge, walk on an even level until you meet the main access road. Turn right to the entrance of the **Jawaharlal Nehru Botanical Gardens**. A trail map depicts the 75 acre (30 hectare) gardens with notations on where to find certain tree and flower types and a glass house holds varieties of Sikkimese orchids. You could easily spend an hour or two roaming through this well-preserved temperate (1,700 m, 5,500 ft) forest.

The drive back to Gangtok weaves down through a pastoral landscape of sculpted paddies and well tended farmhouses, crossing the **Rongni Chu** (or Rani Khola) River and climbing to join the national highway 12 km (7 miles) from Gangtok. It can be difficult to arrange a one-way taxi from Rumtek back to Gangtok, so it is wise to request the taxi which brought you to wait or to return at a fixed time. If you plan to spend the night, there are several simple lodges with basic accommodation and Nepalese or Tibetan style meals. You can also inquire about a ride to the highway (12 km, 7 miles) with one of the early morning local milk delivery jeeps and hail a group jeep from there. Package tours of Rumtek include both ways transport.

Stag dance ushers in the New Year at Rumtek

North Sikkim

A day trip out of Gangtok takes you to the three hillside monasteries of Phodang, Phensang and Labrang. Take a packed lunch and spend the day in the land of the Lepchas and steep forests of North Sikkim.

More than half of the state lies in North Sikkim, an untamed land defined by high Himalayan peaks and passes that only the hardiest pilgrims and traders cross to Tibet. Alpine lakes and oozing glaciers fill high moonscape valleys. The **Tista River,** north-south artery of Sikkim's lifeblood, flushes glacial melt on a tumultuous journey through rhododendron forests clinging to precipitous slopes.

Few outsiders have seen northernmost Sikkim; only a handful of 19th century explorers penetrated the area, today heavily guarded by Indian military posts. Foreigners are allowed only as far as Sangam while Indians may continue (with permission as part of a conducted tour) to Yumthang, known for its rhododendron groves.

A day excursion to **Phodang Monastery** gives a hint of the north's grandeur and is well worth the two to three hour drive. Arrange for a taxi or jeep to ply the 90 km (56 mile) round-trip. Or take the SNT 8 a.m. bus for Mangan, get off below Phodang and walk the half hour up to the monastery. Be back on the main road by 2.30 p.m. (check the current pickup time with the bus driver) or you may miss the last bus to Gangtok.

On the crest of the watershed divide 8 km (5 mile) north of Gangtok, your driver will instinctively stop at **Tashi View Point**. Look north over the Dik Chu tributary of the mighty Tista and in clear weather, northwesterly to-

Masked Kagyat dances at Phodang

ward Kangchendzonga and **Siniolchu** (6,888 m, 22,598 ft), rising ethereally above the valley mists. The road meanders down through lush greenery, terraced farmlands and stilted village houses. Finally, after yet another bend in the road, you reach Phodang Monastery.

Built in 1740, Phodang was Sikkim's leading Kargyudpa centre

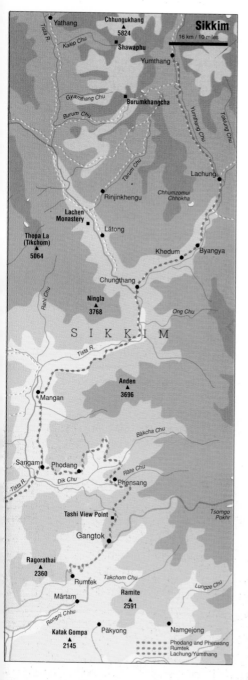

until Rumtek claimed prominence in the 1960s. It is still considered one of the six main monasteries and, along with Rumtek and Ralong, hosts the annual **Kagyat dances** in December.

As with all traditional Sikkimese *gompas* the ornate vestibule shelters paintings of Buddhism's four **Guardians** of the universe. They can be identified by their colours of dress; the white one is from the east, the yellow from the south, red from the west, and green from the north (with occasional variations). Often sharing the entryway is the **Wheel of Life**, a pictorial expression of the Buddha's design for escaping the suffering of endless rebirths and attaining *nirvana*. It is easy to read even without explanation, so apparent is the misery of the poor souls banished to the hellish realms and the bliss of pampered occupants of the palatial heavenly abode. The circular shape represents the ceaseless round of earthly existence, centring on animals symbolising the **Three Original Sins**; a pig for stupidity, surmounted by a snake portraying anger, topped by a cockerel for lust. If a person can avoid these three sins, he or she accumulates merit and virtue and achieves a better chance at being reborn in one of the higher realms. After studying the frescoes, climb upstairs for a view over the tree tops and listen to sounds of monks practising ritual horn playing or reading aloud the holy scripts. The guest house standing near the driveway is for official visitors only.

If you have the time, be sure to visit **Labrang Monastery,** located about 4 km (2.5 miles) up a rocky dirt road above Phodang. Its architecture is quite unusual; the exterior shape is an octagon, built of mortar and brick, sparing an outer coat of plaster and painted rust colour. Take a moment to be aware of the soundlessness, to contemplate a life spent in peaceful meditation far away from traffic and urban din.

Return to the main road and in your taxi continue another 30-40 minutes, around a few more bends, to the small settlement of **Sangam**. If you have no packed lunch you can order *dal bhaat* with chicken or vegetable curry here at the Yak and Yeti Hotel, or stop for a refreshing glass of tea or a cold drink. Sangam is little more than a widening in the road but provides a peek into the lives of rural Sikkimese. Many of the people of this region and northward are Lepchas, the original inhabitants of Sikkim.

The last monastery visit is to **Phensang,** located above the road between Phodang and Gangtok, marked by a cluster of prayer flags. The fourth Chogyal of Sikkim, Gyurmed Namgyal, was to firmly establish the Kargyudpa sect in Sikkim by constructing monasteries at Ralong, Rumtek, Phodang and this one in 1721 at Phensang. The name means "Excellent Banner" or "Good Bliss" and the present monastery replaces the original one which went up in flames in 1947. At times as many as 300 monks are in residence here, though they see relatively few visitors and are both shy and curious.

From Phensang, it is a little more than an hour's drive back to Gangtok. After a long day on the road, you will enjoy a cup of Sikkim's delicious tea or a glass of native-brewed beer. As to dinner plans; the Norkhill Hotel prepares a special Sikkimese dinner and dance programme with one day's advance notice. For groups of at least 15 with prior notice, Sikkim Tourism at the Tourist Information Centre can also arrange an evening of traditional dance.

A fresh shave

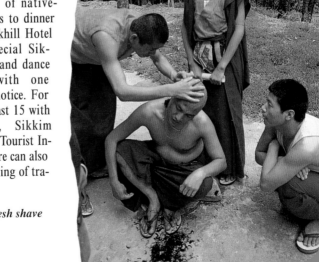

EXCURSIONS

West Sikkim is the gateway to the Himalaya, whether trekking to the base of Kangchendzonga or viewing the mountains from your hotel window. Well tended trails offer easy day hikes while furnished huts ease the rigours of wilderness hiking.

For the less energetic traveller, West Sikkim holds much of historical and cultural interest. Close to Pemayangtse, supreme monastery of Sikkim, stand ruins of the first palace. Tashiding Monastery, with its sin-cleansing *chortens*, rests high above the rivers' confluence.

Traversing a terrain more vertical than anywhere in the tropical Himalaya, paved and well-graded roads snake up and down thou-

A life of meditation

sands of vertical feet in a marvel of engineering. Tourist amenities such as money changing, telephone and health services are limited. Buses run regularly and jeeps can be hired at major centres.

A handful of towns offer simple food and lodging for the independent traveller while comfortable, even deluxe, government hotels and guesthouses serve group tourists. Foreigners must obtain a permit to visit West Sikkim.

Spend three to five days (or more) exploring West Sikkim by vehicle, with optional day hikes in the hills. Your base is the attractive Mount Pandim Hotel at Pemayangtse, whose nearby monastery shelters a unique rainbowed three dimensional sculpture of paradise.

Drive or hike to sacred Kechepari Lake, from where a day hike or two hour drive leads to Yuksom, starting point for treks to higher reaches. Return to Gangtok or leave Sikkim directly to Darjeeling or Siliguri.

Temi Tea And Tenacious Terrain

Drive from Gangtok to Pemayangtse stopping at tea gardens and lookouts on Mount Kangchendzonga. Overnight at the delightful Mount Pandim Hotel, sharing the hilltop with Pemayangtse Monastery.

Pack your bags with good walking shoes and a pair of binoculars and head south from Gangtok to **Singtam**, a transit point close to the main border crossing of Rangpo.

The approximately 130 km (80 mile) drive to Pemayangtse will take about five hours, not including stops, so bring a pack lunch as to dine on local food (*dal bhaat* or *momos*) along the way takes too long.

From Singtam turn west, cross the wide Tista River and enter South Sikkim. The route now twists and turns for 32 km (20 miles) up to **Temi** where Sikkim's prize tea is grown and processed.

If you get an early start from Gangtok (two hours away), you can see the **Temi Tea Estate** in action. Every morning (8.30-11.30 a.m.) tea leaves freshly plucked from the surrounding gardens are brought in for "withering", rolling, sifting, drying and grading, before packaging on the spot.

Tea aroma fills the air. Ask the manager for a guided tour and even a taste of Sikkim's world renowned tea. Boxes of "Temi", "Sikkim Solja" and "Kangchendzonga" pure leaf and blended teas are sold at the estate.

The air cools refreshingly as the road continues upward, leaving the lanky alder, twisted screwpines and countless ferns behind and entering groves of cedar, pines and rhododendron.

At **Damthang** the road divides; one turns south to Namchi, district headquarters, and the other continues west, carving its way across high rock cliffs (13 km, 8 miles) to the small valley rim town of **Rabongla**.

Get out at Rabongla's main intersection and stretch your legs with a two minutes climb to the Department of Forests Bungalow for a clear-shot view of Kangchendzonga.

Just behind the bungalow is the **Kumphenling Tibetan Refugee**

Pemayangtse Monastery, housing seven levels of "paradise"

Centre with a small *gompa*. Approximately 900 Tibetan refugees live here, some of whom produce traditional handicrafts, particularly carpets, for sale in Gangtok. Regulations prohibit foreigners from entering the Refugee Centre without permission from the Central Government Home Ministry in New Delhi.

Look southwest from Rabongla toward Damthang, and you see the hilltop of **Tendong**, of legendary significance. The Sikkimese tell of a time when this cloud-capped land lay beneath the sea — coincidental with geologic history — and Tendong stuck its head just above the water.

A neighbouring hilltop called Bale Dhunga (Rooster Rock), the triple hump ridge east of Rabongla, was slipping into the water and called to Tendong for help. The latter advised Bale Dunga to strain and raise up its sinking head and neck, thus raising itself to a dominant height, as it remains today.

Locals also recount that the *migue*, Sikkimese for the abominable snowman or yeti, lives high on Bale Dhunga and thrashes the walls and doors of a ridgetop monastery so loudly that *lamas* cannot complete their meditation retreat there.

A trail leads from Damthang through forest to the flat top of Tendong (less than two hours mod-

The Tista snakes through lush greenery

erately easy walking uphill) where an old lama tends a small *gompa*. In clear weather, you can see all the way to the Terai and much of South Sikkim. Watch for orchids along the trail during late spring.

At Rabongla, the road crosses a major divide and descends about 1,000 meters (3,300 ft) to the **Rangit River**. On the way down, you sight several monasteries dotting the rolling hillsides; on the left side of the road at Kewzing is **Kundragling Monastery**, the only Bon monastery in Sikkim.

Bon is the animist pre-Buddhist religion of Tibet. Bonpo, or people of the Bon faith, walk around their holy places in a counter-clockwise direction, opposite to Buddhists and decorate hilltops with cairns and flags.

As the road makes long sweeps across the hillside, passengers on both sides of the vehicle will have plenty of opportunity to view Tashiding Monastery perched at the tiptop of a conical hill opposite. Visitors to Tashiding must get prior permission from Sikkim Tourism at the Tourism Information Centre in Gangtok, or a trekking permit will suffice.

The Rangit marks your entrance to West Sikkim, and a guard

Some of the best tea in the world

post at Legship checks your authorization. Wind your way up the switchbacks to **Geyzing**, district headquarters, and straight up another 7 km (4.3 miles) to Pemayangtse and the **Mount Pandim Hotel**. Set at a cool 2,076 m (6,800 ft), the hotel affords sweeping views of the snow covered Himalaya; supreme Kangchendzonga, flanked by Kabur, Talong, Kokthang and Narsingh (Mount Pandim itself is hidden by others.) Every room has a spectacular view, and from the gardens you can scout the next few days' excursions in every direction.

The Mount Pandim Hotel is by far the most luxurious abode available, but for budget travellers there is a Trekkers' Hut with dormitory accommodations, and several small private hotels in Geyzing.

A Tangible Paradise At Pemayangtse

After sunrise on the Himalaya, walk 15 minutes from your hotel to Pemayangtse Monastery. After lunch take an afternoon hike to Sangacholing Monastery or to Rabdentse Palace Ruins. Enjoy a Sikkimese cultural programme in the evening.

Rise early for a clear weather view of the mountains. Morning is also the best time to visit **Pemayangtse Monastery**, a short walk or five minute drive away.

Pemayangtse – which means "the Sublime Perfect Lotus" signifying purity – was originally built as a small *lhakhang* in the early 17th century by Gewala Lhatsun Chempo, one of the three Tibetan *lamas* who gathered at Yuksom in 1642 to choose Sikkim's first Chogyal.

There is a statue of him inside behind the altar, to the right of the central figure Guru Rinpoche, or Padmasambhava. The *lhakhang* was later expanded during the third Chogyal's reign in the early 18th century by a reincarnation of Lhatsun Chempo. It is paramount of the Nyingmapa monasteries and regarded as Sikkim's most prestigious centre of religious learning.

Wall frescoes have taken on muted colours of medieval oils and an oversize *thangka* rests ready to be unfurled at the annual Guru Drag-dmar *chaam* ceremony held two days before Losar.

Devotees come from throughout Sikkim to witness the Pemayangtse *lamas* perform dance rituals, dressed in magnificent costumes and masks.

Ask a monk to show you the way upstairs. Encased in ceiling high glass is a seven level wooden pagoda structure of mind-boggling intricacy depicting paradise – Sangthokpalri – or Guru Rinpoche's celestial palace.

Crafted exclusively by

the late Dungzin Rinpoche over five years, this masterpiece contains countless miniature painted figures. Skeletons and beings from hell are on the bottom level, then tigers and beasts among green sculpted hills and tiny birds in trees, superseded by a human realm, then several levels of holy existence adorned with small *chortens*, standing Buddhas, flying garudas and dragons suspended from the roofs' corners. It is indeed a unique creation, never to be forgotten (and not to be photographed).

After lunch take a walk to **Sangacholing Monastery**. Founded by Lhatsun Chempo in 1697, Sangacholing was damaged by fire and replaced within the last 30 years with the present *gompa*. Some of the 17th century clay statues were restored and are amongst the oldest preserved in Sikkim.

A gentle trail winds down along a ridge for about 4 km (2.5 miles) to the site; it is easily reached in 60-90 minutes and back in the same amount of time.

Ask the hotel manager to head you in the right direction or to provide a local guide who will be able to point out important sites along the way; the hoof-print of Guru Rinpoche's horse and a stone said to have been used by Lhatsun Chempo as a meditation seat.

An alternative afternoon walk – or to save for another day – leaves from above Geyzing bazaar for **Rabdentse Palace Ruins**, about a kilometre away.

Take a local guide as there are several trails from which to choose. Little remains of Sikkim's second capital, moved here from Yuksom during the late 17th century, but some crumbled stone walls at an overgrown site.

Be back home in time for sunset. For evening entertainment; a good book in your snug room or for something more lively, ask the hotel in advance to arrange a dance performance exhibiting costumes and steps in the Sikkimese as well as Tibetan, Lepcha and Nepalese traditions.

The traditional Sikkimese house

A Leafless Lake And A Taste Of Trekking

Drive from Pemayangtse through terraced hills to Kechepari Lake and a hillside monastery. Continue by road to Yuksom and overnight there, or return to Pemayangtse.

The Sikkimese, like their cousins the Tibetans, love family picnics. They combine a day or overnight with a pilgrimage to a sacred place, gaining merit toward a good future life. Old and young join in the food preparation and after a few rounds of fermented rice or barley *chhang*, laughter, singing and dancing take over. Then everyone piles back into the rented vehicle and the songs and jokes continue all the way home.

Kechepari Lake is a favourite picnic-pilgrimage place for the Sikkimese. Nestled in a forested bowl at around 2,000 m (6,500 ft), it also boasts an extraordinary legend; whenever a leaf drops towards its surface, a guardian bird snatches it away. Indeed you won't see a single floating leaf, odd since it is surrounded by trees.

From Pemayangtse, the road weaves west then north along hillsides planted with alder-shaded cardamon fields. Black cardamon is Sikkim's chief export, the pods used to spice Indian curries but rarely found in Sikkimese food. Standing up to 2 m (6 ft) tall, the plant's bunches of blades hide small yellow flowers which precede the pods. Tending the wet slopes during monsoon is the farmer's dreaded job, the muddy ground crawling with leeches and the occasional snake.

Pass through the small town of Rimbi. Descend beneath waterfalls to the turn-off to Kechepari; you will continue along the main road toward Yuksom later in the day. The Rimbi powerhouse harnesses one of the many rivers draining the high Himalaya, its water chute and turbine set opposite an impressive suspension bridge. Like Sikkim's roads, the bridges are an engineering feat vital to transport and communication in these telephone-less rural areas.

Kechepari Lake – draped in prayer flags but not a leaf

The unpaved road up to Kechepari Lake (about 11 km, 7 miles) is a good example of a cliff-hanger, though well maintained. You reach the lake in an hour or two. Locals believe that once you set out for Kechepari, you must not turn back or bad luck will result. As the road makes its last gentle turn approaching the Trekkers' Hut, look off to the right (northeast) and see Kangchendzonga on the horizon. Not a sound but birdsong fills the silence.

A gentle reminder

Walk 15 minutes up a wide shaded path. Soon the lake appears on the left, its glassy surface bordered with reeds. A wood walkway passes a small shelter where well-wishers may light a butter lamp. Tall prayer flags lend a festive air, the only colour in the natural landscape. Show your respect of this holy place by not smoking, talking loudly or spoiling the environment. Linger awhile, scanning the waters for that little caretaker bird. If time permits, ask the driver to point the way up to the monastery, set high on the slope above the Trekkers' Hut, from where Yuksom may be visible.

Once on the main road, **Yuksom** lies about an hour's drive away. An alternative is to walk there with a guide. You can make the 8 km (5 miles) walk through thick shrubbery and Lepcha villages in a quick half day or leisurely full day. You may also hike all the way from Pemayangtse via Kechepari, overnighting at the hut and be picked up at Yuksom the next day. No trekking permit is necessary.

Like Kechepari, Yuksom sits in the lap of a gentle valley but one that opens north onto the Dzongri trek route. Approaching the end of the road past a high school, a couple of private lodges offer simple meals and rooms. Continue another mile to the upper bazaar, where there is a Police Checkpost and the Yuksom Trekkers' Hut, located off the road to the left. Styled like a Swiss chalet with flower gardens and cows grazing in the meadows, it is a delightful retreat with double, triple and dormitory rooms and an indoor bathroom with shower. If a cook is around, meals might be prepared on request, or else place your order at the friendly Hotel Dzongrila next to the Police post. A trekking permit is needed to continue on from here.

If the comforts of the Mount Pandim Hotel have you in their grip, drive back to the hilltop oasis along the same route through Rimbi. Or, if rooms are available and your driver is willing to wait overnight (for a fee), spend the night at Yuksom Trekkers' Hut and explore this historic vale the next day. You can make reservations at the Yuksom Hut with an agent or Sikkim Tourism in Gangtok.

Yuksom, Cradle Of Sikkim

Day walk to the site of the first Chogyal's enthronement and peek up the valley toward Dzongri trek route. Overnight in rustic comfort at the Trekkers' Hut.

Among the many pleasures of Sikkim are the *dak* bungalows, remnants of the British Raj when visiting officers preferred a roof between their gins and the stars. The tradition has carried over in **Trekkers' Huts**. Beginning at the village of Yuksom, Trekkers' Huts are spaced four to six hours' walk apart, inviting the less intrepid camper to experience outdoor living.

But even the non-trekker can get a taste of Sikkim trekking with a day hike in the woods, visiting historic spots and scenic viewpoints, overnighting in Yuksom. An abundance of village cows assures fresh milk tea for breakfast and at the Yuksom Trekkers' Hut you can read about some 40 varieties of Himalayan rhododendron. If it's springtime you will see a few at these lower elevations; there are greater concentrations on high. Be sure to check in at the Police Checkpost to let them know your plans.

A botanists' paradise

Ask about hiring a local guide to show the way to ridgetop **Dubdi Monastery**, after Sangacholing the oldest monastery in Sikkim built in about 1701. Thread your way up through dense forest cleared at the lower reaches for cultivation of corn and millet. It's a steady one and a half hour walk up a good 300 m (1,000 ft) to the monastery.

The effort is rewarded with a view of Yuksom vale stretching before this perfect hermitage site. Like all monasteries, it may be locked if monks are away on duty, so be sure to ask your guide before setting out if seeing the *gompa*'s interior is a priority. Bring a snack and some water – and some salt to remove leeches in the rainy season – and recall the history of this "Gathering Place of Three Superior Ones" as Yuksom translates, where the three Tibetan lamas met and crowned the first Chogyal of Sikkim in 1642.

Far below, looking west, you can see the **Norbugang Chorten** where Lhatsun Chempo buried offerings given by the people to their new Chogyal. After descending from Dubdi, a gentle half hour walk from the Trekkers' Hut leads to the a large stone which served at Chogyal Phuntsog Namgyal's throne.

Just in front of it stands another *chorten* which the consecrating

Trekking in style, a choice of tent or "hut"

lamas built with stones and earth from all parts of Sikkim to hold religious treasures presented by Lhatsun Chempo for the goodwill of Sikkim and world peace. A shorter day outing would take in just the *chorten* and throne sites and leave Dubdi monastery to the fleetfooted and energetic.

Check in for another quiet evening at the Trekkers' Hut, or drive back to Pemayangtse in time for dinner. Daily buses run between Yuksom and Pemayangtse but only in the morning.

Sikkim To Darjeeling - A Corrugated Ocean Of Tea

Bid farewell to Sikkim and greet Darjeeling where the British Raj found relief in highland breezes and clubhouse gatherings.

A final departure from Pemayangtse hill descends some 1,000 m (3,300 ft) to **Legship,** overlooking the Rangit River. Here a polite checkpost officer dutifully glances in every passing car for foreign tourists and asks for the proper West Sikkim permit. Your route follows the Rangit's steep banks south past a hydro-electric facility and the popular mineral hotsprings at **Chachu.**

By bus or jeep, you reach the trade junction of **Jorethang** in one and a half to two hours. Follow the locals to the respectable and reasonably-priced Namgyal Hotel for a cool drink or an instant plate of beef *momos,* served with fresh tomato-chili sauce. Rooms are available at several lodges should you get in late.

Tea, Darjeeling's raison d'stre

If travelling independently, you can arrange here for custom or group jeeps to Namchi or other major destinations of Sikkim; or on to Darjeeling and beyond. Scout out a sturdy vehicle to make the tedious three hour 27 km (17 mile) drive to Darjeeling.

Or Yuksom To Gangtok Via Tashiding

Tashiding Monastery, with its sin-cleansing *chorten* **and holy water vessel is one of the most sacred spots of Sikkim.**

After an overnight in Yuksom, you need not return to Pemayangtse but can drive to Gangtok in seven to eight hours, visiting **Tashiding Monastery** en route. Occasionally jeeps are available for rent at Yuksom or can be ordered a day in advance. It is best before departing Pemayangtse to ask the Mount Pandim manager to arrange a jeep to pick you up and take you to Gangtok.

A well maintained dirt road weaves across high cliffs and down to a small settlement below Tashiding's pyramid hill in about one and a half hours from Yuksom.

There is a Trekkers' Hut and a campsite available here; some trekking groups extend their walking tour from Yuksom, reaching here in two days. Leave the vehicle at a narrow saddle and walk about 40 minutes up to the monastery; a jeep can drive up further, shortening the walk to 20-30 minutes.

A newly constructed *gompa* straddles a flat hilltop, replacing the

Trekkers' Huts are available up to 3,800 m (12,500 ft)

original one built some 360 years ago by Ngadak Sempa Chempo at a spot where a rainbow connected with Kangchendzonga. More buildings were added under the reign of Sikkim's third Chogyal (around 1717) making this one of the earliest Nyingmapa sites. Sikkim's last reigning Chogyal Palden Thondup Namgyal instigated the building of the new monastery, preserving some of the old supporting beams and statues.

Tashiding is best known for its *chortens,* clustered on a promontory jutting hundreds of meters above the confluence of the Rangit and Ratong Rivers. The central monument is the holiest, said to cleanse its beholder of all sins – hence its name which means "Saviour by Mere Sight." Its holiness is due to the contents; some white seed-like granules which remained after the cremation of a predecessor to Sakyamuni Buddha, the prescriber of Buddhism who lived two and a half millennia ago. A wall of unusually large blue *mani* stones circle the *chortens.*

Pilgrims come from throughout Sikkim each year to pay homage at Tashiding on the 15th day of the first Tibetan month (in late February). At this time, holy water called *Bumchu* is dispersed among the devout to guarantee a heavenly next life. Kept in the original 300 year old vessel blessed by Tashiding's founder, the water is said to never dry up. Whether the container is full or half empty signifies good or bad times ahead.

The road zigzags down the south-facing slope and joins the Geyzing-Singtam road on the opposite side of the Rangit River. Note that a visit to Tashiding can also be included en route to Yuksom from Gangtok.

Trekking in Sikkim

With a keenness for country walking and an urgency to escape India's summer heat, the British took to Sikkim's cool hills earlier in this century and became its first foreign trekkers. Rest houses, 29 in all, conveniently situated a day's walk apart along the major trails, certainly took the rigorous edge off of hiking through this vertical terrain.

Trekking has changed little in the last 50 years; Annie Perry's *Kalimpong and the Sikkim Hills: A Guide and Handbook on Touring written in 1949,* still offers relevant advice:

"The essentials for a successful tour is physical fitness. The tourist will be well repaid for his efforts by days spent in the bracing air among hills and mountains, with views of glaciers and the snows and the variety of flowers and trees which cover the slopes. The ideal number for a tour is a party of four persons [Note: present day trekking regulations apparently agree, setting the minimum size of a group at four].

"Seasons: The best months for touring in Sikkim are October/November and December/January. April and May are also good

months though at this time of the year there may be a few showers of rain. The rhododendron flowers are at the best from the May 5 to June 15. In December and January there are liable to be heavy falls of snow at the heights.

"Personnel: If one is on a holiday and not prepared to go into details of arranging porters, mules and in supervising the caravan on tour, it is advisable to engage a Sirdar... The visitor may take his own cook or bearer, but if he is a plainsman and not used to the heights, it is better to leave him behind as he will probably turn out more of a liability than an asset."

It is unlikely today that foreign trekkers need ponder whether to bring their own cook or bearer, encumbered with worries over the plainsman's adaptability. Nowadays, all of that is handled by a trekking company which arranges every detail for you.

Trekkers of the 1990s may next ask, "How is trekking in Sikkim different from in Nepal?". In Sikkim, trekkers are not allowed to roam unaccompanied through the hills as in Nepal. Foreigners must form a group of at least four persons and support services must be arranged through a registered trekking agency in Sikkim.

But surprisingly, given the two country's juxtaposition, the scenery is quite different. Because of a generous monsoon compounded by a relatively low population density and strict controls on timber cutting, Sikkim's forests are still largely intact and contain marvellous varieties of vegetation. Flowering trees and plants, ferns, vines, mushrooms and mosses support a colourful menagerie of birds, butterflies, moths and large and small mammals. Along Sikkim's trekking trails dwellings are scant, though smoke rises from a handful of cow and yak herders' huts and summer grazing settlements.

There are five trekking routes open to foreign and Indian trekkers in West and South Sikkim, and when North Sikkim opens, even more. Only two, however, consistently stay away from roads; the **Rhododendron Trek** (an easy two to three days) and the **Dzongri to Kangchendzonga Trek** (a moderately difficult seven to ten days). The other three routes, the **Orchid Trek**, the **Coronation Trek** and the **Youth (or Country) Trek** are used primarily by Indian school groups and spend much time walking on drivable roads.

A novel innovation along the Sikkim trails is the dry shelter afforded by Trekkers' Huts, spaced a day's walk apart. Not every trekker appreciates sleeping within walls, however, and for some the sounds of wind and running water outside the tent are more comforting. State your preference upon signing up for the trek. In either case, latrines and refuse pits at every night's stop means that trails and campsites are largely free of waste.

Indian tourists may trek independently without a guide, but they must check in with trailhead managers to be sure that they are adequately equipped with food and warm clothing. A nominal

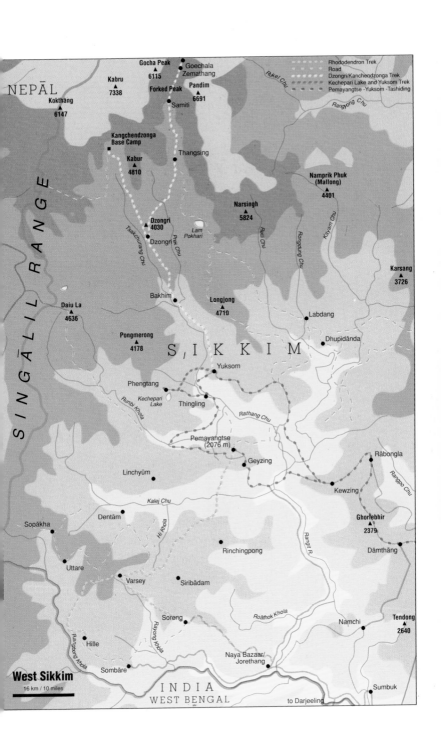

NEPĀL

SINGĀLIL RANGE

Kokthāng
▲
6147

Kabru
▲
7338

Gocha Peak
▲
6115

Goechala
Zemathang

Forked Peak
Samiti

Pandim
▲
6691

Rikel Chu

Rangyong Chu

Kangchendzonga
Base Camp

Kabur
▲
4810

Thangsing

Namprik Phuk
(Mallong)
▲
4401

Dzongri
▲
4030
Dzongri

Tsakchuang Chu

Prek Chu

Lam
Pokhari

Narsingh
▲
5824

Reili Chu

Rangdung Chu

Kayam Chu

Karsang
▲
3726

Bakhim

Longjong
▲
4710

Labdang

Daiu La
▲
4636

Pongmerong
▲
4178

Dhupidānda

S I K K I M

Yuksom

Phengtang

Kechepari
Lake

Thingling

Rathang Chu

Runbi Khola

Pemayangtse
(2076 m)

Geyzing

Rābongla

Rangpo Chu

Linchyūm

Kewzing

Kalej Chu

Hi Khola

Ghorlebhir
▲
2379

Sopākha

Dentām

Rangit R.

Dāmthāng

Uttare

Rinchingpong

Varsey

Siribādam

Rayong Khola

Soreng

Roathok Khola

Namchi

Tendong
▲
2640

Rangpong Khola

Hille

Sombāre

Naya Bazaar/
Jorethang

Sumbuk

West Sikkim
16 km / 10 miles

I N D I A
WEST BENGAL

to Darjeeling

Rhododendron Trek
Road
Dzongri/Kanchendzonga Trek
Kechepari Lake and Yuksom Trek
Pemayangtse - Yuksom - Tashiding

trekking fee is requested, as well as sleeping charges at each of the Trekkers' Huts. Tents can be rented from Sikkim Tourism at some trailheads. Porters or yaks (with drivers) can be hired at Yuksom for a set daily wage.

Rhododendron Trek

A four or six day trek with short and easy days of walking visiting prime rhododendron forests, vibrant with colour in spring.

The Rhododendron Trek through the southwest corner of Sikkim is ideal for first-time trekkers. It follows gentle terrain (with inevitably some ups and downs) and short hiking days. There are variations to the route, depending upon how much or little you want to walk.

Firs and rhododendrons cover higher slopes

At these elevations, around 2,000 m (6,500 ft), the best time to see the rhododendrons in full bloom is from the end of March through mid-May. A brief sample itinerary which could be added on to any Sikkim visit might read as follows.

Drive to Jorethang (from Rangpo entry post, Gangtok, Bagdogra/Siliguri or Darjeeling) and stay overnight there in simple lodgings. On the second day, drive from Jorethang west to Hille and hike one and a half to two hours through prime rhododendron groves to Varsey. Overnight in a Trekkers' Hut which has solar-powered electricity. The third day's hike is a moderately easy half-day stretch easterly to Soreng through dense clusters of rhododendrons. Overnight in a Trekkers' Hut and on the fourth day drive to

Pemayangtse or Gangtok.

If you are doing a six day excursion, continue trekking from Soreng through Kaluk and Rinchenpong to Dentam, and then drive to Pemayangtse. When not amidst the rhododendron, you will be traversing low hills, many under cultivation with corn, rice or millet.

Dzongri And Kangchendzonga Trek

Unrivalled as a high altitude trek anywhere in the Himalaya is the seven to ten day hike to Dzongri and Goechela, with an alternative trip to Kangchendzonga Base Camp.

Views onto the snow-bound Himalaya are quickly gained on the Dzongri and Kangchendzonga treks, but at a cost – quick and steep ascents of 1,200 m (4,000 ft) elevation gain in the first day. Higher up, hanging snowfields plaster every mountaintop and at night zillions of stars fill the crisp skies. This trek combines the best of all worlds.

Even though it is the best and most popular trek in Sikkim, it is not overrun nor cluttered with Coke signs and tea stalls. For every night's halt, there are designated campsites and huts with latrines and refuse pits; government regulations require trekking groups to cook on kerosene to preserve the forests in their natural state.

For veterans of Nepal trails, the Dzongri and Kangchendzonga trek might be compared to the Annapurna Sanctuary trek in difficulty, and to a combination of Langtang and Everest in scenery. The initial elevation gain is strenuous – from 1,780 m to 3,050 m (5,840 ft - 10,000 ft) the first day, and up another 1,000 m (3,300 ft) the next – then levelling off with a gradual ascent to just over 5,000 m (16,400 ft) at Goechela. In the upper reaches, you hike up a long glaciated valley rimmed with snow-capped peaks and camp beneath the half-dome of Mount Pandim (6,691 m, 21,925 ft). Many of these peaks remain unclimbed and are deemed sacred by the Sikkimese people.

The trek usually begins at Yuksom, but to help get stagnant muscles used to the terrain, some companies suggest a warm-up day or two's hike from Kechepari Lake. At Yuksom, the trail turns north and disappears into mist rising from the Ratong Chu (*chu* means both water and river in Sikkimese language). Undulating through forests of oak, alder, walnut and cedar, resonating with cricket shrills and lively bird calls, the trail crosses three side streams over sturdy wooden bridges and then the Prek Chu before launching an hour or two's steep ascent up the opposite bank. As throughout the whole trek, trails are well-maintained, with plenty of switchbacks.

En route to **Bakhim** or preferably **Tsokha** (five to six hours) you are likely to encounter herders with their yaks and cows. Dairy products are a major part of the Sikkimese diet, served as rich milk tea, or cooked and set aside in wooden containers called *theaki* to make delicious thick yogurt. Every morning, from any hill farmer's kitchen you may hear the splashing sound of butter being churned in a tall wooden cylinder (*kyodong*). The remaining buttermilk makes a refreshing drink, or is again cooked, separating into fresh grainy cheese (*chhurpi*) which is hung in squares from the ceiling to dry or heated with spices and butter and served with the meal. *Chhurpi* and *tsampa* (finely ground roasted barley, rice or corn) consumed with butter tea or *chhang* are the staples of every high altitude household and Himalayan trader, good for energy and easy to store. Ask your trekking guide if you can sample some.

Yaks share a trekkers' camp above treeline

The forest opens up at the one-house settlement of Bakhim, with its spacious dormitory hostel. But the setting is more favourable one hour (and 300 m, 1,000 ft) further at Tsokha, worth the extra effort unless you are feeling light-headed or short-winded from the altitude. Clinging to a forested hillside, no more than fifteen wooden houses make up Tsokha. An unpretentious new *gompa* overlooks the "town" next to a pond festooned with prayer flags. From the campsite, the Himalaya make their first appearance towering above the gorge, while down-valley the lights of Yuksom and distant Darjeeling can be seen. If time permits, wonder amidst the herders' summer homes. If asked to come in and sit down, remember not to point your feet at the host or any sacred objects, and to respect privacy if photographing.

Day two's walk to **Dzongri** is nothing short of magical. A wooden plank path leads through a wonderland of tangled rhododendron branches and misshapen firs draped in wisps of Spanish moss. If you are willing to risk a bit of rain, come in mid-May for the most beautiful flower show you will ever see. Between Tsokha

and Dzongri, the hillsides are painted in pink, red, white, yellow and lavender as different varieties of rhododendrons fade in and out of flower. Huge clusters of watermelon red blossoms light up trees 9 m to 15 m (30-50 ft) tall, framing the shady path at around 3,500 m (11,500 ft). **Phedang Meadows** (today's lunch stop) are edged in yellow trumpet blossoms and bouquets of crimson red, pale pink and ivory. The afternoon's hike (one hour steep climb after lunch) breaks treeline at a *deorali* (high point) decorated in auspicious prayer flags and rides a ridge covered in yellow and violet rhododendron shrubs before descending slightly to Dzongri (4,030 m, 13,222 ft). The total walking time is five to six hours.

Day three is set aside to rest and acclimatise at Dzongri, the take-off point to Kangchendzonga Base Camp. Snuggled against the protective height of Dzongri peak, the camp site is somewhat sheltered against cold winds and heavy fog which drive up the tributary valley of Tsakchurang Chu. This is where the two trails split; north to Goechela or northwest to Kangchendzonga Base Camp. A three to four day walk to Base Camp and back exposes the hardy adventurer to less-trodden ground, and glaciers tumbling off of Kokthang, Ratong and Kabru peaks. As from many expeditionary base camps, Kangchendzonga itself is not visible from the valley floor but can be seen from high points en route.

Mammoth mountains rise to both sides

No matter where you are bound, it is wise – imperative unless you have recently been hiking above 3,000 m (10,000 ft) – to spend a day (two nights) at Dzongri for altitude acclimatization. As all high altitude specialists will tell you, it is best to be somewhat active on your "rest" day; take a day hike, as rigorous as you feel up to, to higher ground and return to Dzongri to sleep. This will actually help your body adjust to the thin air. A couple of day-hike suggestions are:

Rise early and climb Dzongri peak (one hour) for an unforgettable sunrise over Mount Pandim,

Glaciers pushing onto Goechela

Kabru, Tinchenkhang, Kabur and the Kangchendzonga range. You can trace the trek route onward toward Goechela and look east toward Lam Pokhari ("Long Lake") a good day hike destination out of Thangsing. Carry tea to drink in small bunkers built into the sandy hilltop (about 4,600 m, 14,000 ft; it never tasted so good. Descend for breakfast.

Later in the morning, set off for Lakshmi Pokhari, another alpine lake, this one named for the Hindu goddess of wealth. It is set at the base of black Kabur, a minor jagged peak which challenges the rock climber seeking bird's eye views of the higher mountains. From Dzongri peak, set off in a northerly direction across the meadows and stay high to the left above the main trail which descends right to the Prek Chu. You will need a guide to find the lake, and should plan on two to three hours to reach it. Bring a pack lunch.

For a gentler outing, wander up the trail to the left of Dzongri peak and continue toward some herders' stone *goths* (summer shelters), exploring the slopes scented with dwarf rhododendron, picked and dried for religious incense, called *sunpati*.

The trek on day four reaches Thangsing or Samiti. Well rested, proceed over the east shoulder of Dzongri peak and cross rambling terrain, stopping frequently to gaze upon the stunning line-up of Himalayan peaks. Mount Pandim and Kabru dominate the foreground left and right of the Prek Chu valley, while Kangchendzonga takes backstage, its light-coloured sharp summit tapering to the east. What a different profile than the broad, chunky rounded face seen from Nepal.

Now the trail takes a steeper angle and descends into a band of rhododendron forest briefly repeating the command performance of two days ago. This is the only major elevation loss of this trek, ending at the edge of a broad rocky river bed whose newly built bridges and widely strewn boulders tell the story of a recent flood. Pick your way up the

Mt. Pandim commands the skyline

west side and cross the wooden bridge, then traverse a lovely fir forest and follow the creek to **Thangsing** (3,800 m, 12,467 ft), set at the bottom of Tinchenkhang and a long glacial valley. The walking time from Dzongri is three to four hours.

Some groups stop here, soaking up the natural high in the afternoon sun. Another three hours will see you beyond Thangsing's last Trekkers' Hut to **Samiti Lake** (4,060 m, 13,320 ft). The first half is a gradual climb alongside a milky stream, breaking into steeper slopes at a lone yak herders' hut. You are now walking on the lateral moraine of a gigantic glacier. The trail again crosses high grasslands and picks its way through lichen covered boulders, the mountains closing in on both sides as the valley narrows.

At last, the campsite is visible just minutes away at the shore of emerald coloured Lake Samiti. A rock house serves as the cooks' shelter, or can sleep 10 or 12 on a

Skirting moraine and a glacial like on the way to the pass

dirt floor if the weather turns bad. Protected from the ice chilled winds, this small oasis seems far from all the demands of the life you left at home.

On day five you are approaching the climax of the trek, a day trip to **Goechela**, and a few night-before prayers for clear weather are in order. The pass, at about 4,940 m (16,200 ft), lies only four hours walk away but at these elevations it may seem like you will never get there. Though it is hard to drag yourself out of bed into the cold, dark, still air, you will not regret organising a group effort to reach the pass for dawn.

Compared to other Himalayan passes, this one is not difficult but you must go slow and be prepared with warm layers, sun glasses, snack food, drinking water and a hat. The trail parallels the Samiti lake source and crosses rocky moraine overlooking an inlet of ice. After an hour's climb, the route drops down to cross a mammoth sandy lakebed and again mounts a rise before scrambling up again to the top of the moraine. From here the pass looks just minutes away, but at high elevation distances are deceivingly fore-shortened. Piles of rocks mark the way, and the now-familiar summit feature of a cairn with wind-torn prayer flags signals that your upward feat is finished. A massive ice fall on your left defies gravity. Fuzzy cushion plants and copper-coloured algae push life's upper limits, and the imagination soars to what might be seen standing on top of these towering ice and rock ramparts.

North from Goechela's saddle gap the sun ignites Kangchendzonga and Kabru on the west. The silhouette of Mount Pandim with it saw-tooth neighbours splays the sun's golden rays and gives new relief to the drama close at hand.

The way back seems effortless, recalling each laboured upward step. Snow cocks and cuckoos call to the wind. You will be in Samiti within two and a half hours and depending upon the time and weather, can either spend another night there or descend another two and a half hours to Thangsing. The latter makes a long day, and rewards a full rest the next day.

On the sixth day out, sleep late, take a deserved bath (it is best to toss your bath water away from the stream) and catch up on reading or writing. One of the luxuries of trekking is time. The more energetic can hike from Thangsing to Lam Pokhari and back, following the high banks of the Prek Chu.

On day seven return to Tsokha. Retrace your steps to the wooden bridge and follow the trail which you descended from Dzongri uphill for about 10 minutes. A signposted junction shows an alternative route (not open to pack animals) back to Tsokha. It is somewhat shorter, 3½ to 4 hours to Phedang – if that is your lunch stop, take along a snack – and 1½ to two hours to Tsokha, and a gentler grade. The trail stays through rhododendron and fir forest the entire time, weaving in and out of countless stream canyons through tangles of roots and rocks. You sacrifice the last of the mountain views for the thrill of tramping through untamed forest. Arrive in Tsokha by mid-afternoon.

By day eight, the uphill grunts of a week ago seem distant as you descend the same trail, seeing much more with new eyes. You can make it back to Yuksom in five easy hours, returning to the real shower at Trekkers' Hut.

On your last, ninth day, drive to Pemayangtse and conclude your visit to West Sikkim with a restful stay at the Mount Pandim Hotel. Or head back to Gangtok via Tashiding Monastery, reaching the capital in one full day or overnighting in the Tashiding Trekkers' Hut, allowing a more leisurely encounter.

White Water Thrills

Sikkim has just begun offering Himalayan rafting trips, featuring half-day runs on the tempestuous Tista. From the road the waves look moderate in the midst of such a wide expanse of water. But where the rapids narrow the water's force concentrates and some fun rides develop. Life-jackets and helmets are provided and the guides have been instructed in safety.

So far, only one stretch of the lower Tista is open but chances are the upper river will open soon. Boats put in at an army post access near Bardang and float 8 km (5 miles) down to Rangpo, where you can dry off and change clothes at the Rangpo Tourist Lodge, and have lunch before continuing on to Siliguri. Afternoon trips end with dinner and an overnight at Rangpo. Nothing like going out with a splash. Inquire at the Rangpo Tourist Lodge upon entry to Sikkim or with your agent to book your rafting adventure.

Tsangu Lake Snow Day Trip, East Sikkim

(currently permitted for Indian nationals only)

Package trips for Indian tourists venture further afield than foreigners are allowed to go. These excursions are arranged by Sikkim Tourism; private tour operators offer similar trips but must seek permission for tourists to enter the restricted zone. The price includes accommodation, meals and transportation.

A one day drive up and back to Tsangu Lake follows the old trade route east from Gangtok toward Natu La, one of the main passes to Tibet. Snow lingers late into spring, making it a favourite spot for families to romp in the snow. You are surrounded by alpine forests and can glimpse the Himalaya before turning back, returning to Gangtok the same day. At this elevation, close to 3,600 m (11,000 ft), watch for signs of altitude sickness.

Overnight Yumthang Alpine Tour, North Sikkim

(currently permitted for Indian nationals only)

This trip heads north into the Yumthang Valley of Lachung region amidst some prime rhododendron and mixed forest. Leave Gangtok at about 8 a.m. Follow the road past Phodang through Mangan, continuing north paralleling the Tista River to Chungthang. Turn east off the main north-south route and follow the Lachung Valley, reaching your destination by 3 p.m. Stay overnight at a tourist hut which offers dormitory accommodations.

On the second day, drive another hour to Yumthang. The air is markedly cooler here

A rare long-leafed rhododendron of North Sikkim

with mountains creeping in up toward 6,000 m (20,000 ft) on all sides. It is only about 25 km (15 miles) as the crow flies to the Tibet border and the inhabitants, both Lepcha and Tibetans, have a distinctive mountain look. Relax and walk about throughout the morning, and drive the same route back to Gangtok, reaching there by 8 p.m.

DARJEELING

For almost 150 years Darjeeling has been the darling of east Himalayan travellers, where ailing British bureaucrats crossed paths with uncouth Tibetan traders and disguised explorers cum spies prepared for passage to Lhasa. Such a cast of characters only exists on the movie screen these days, but Darjeeling still holds captive a cadre of rookie and returnee visitors charmed by its mountain scenery and quaintly cosmopolitan air. The red tape of special permit requirements is now waived for Darjeeling and Kalimpong, and visitors can stay as long as their India visa allows.

Darjeeling

1 Himalayan Mountaineering Instit.
2 Himalayan Zoological Park
3 Raj Bhawan
4 Tibetan Refugee Centre
5 Bhutia Bustee Monastery
6 Observatory Hill
7 St.Andrew's Church
8 Windamere Hotel
9 New Elgin Hotel
10 Natural History Museum
11 Maples Tourist Lodge
12 Tourist Bureau
13 Indian Airlines
14 Capitol Theatre

Passenger Ropeway

15 Telegraph Office
16 Youth Hostel
17 Aloobari Buddhist Monastery
18 Mt. Everest Hotel
19 Ava Art Gallery
20 Dhirdham Temple
21 Railway Station
22 G.P.O.
23 Lloyd Botanical Garden
24 Loreto Convent
25 Eden Hospital
26 Tourist Lodge

= = = Darjeeling
= = = Chowrastha
= = = Ghoom and Tigerhill

Not to Scale

To Singla
To Bijanbari
Rangnit Tea Estate
Gorkha Stadium
Lebong Cart Rd
C. R. Das Rd
Jawahar Rd. W.
Pandam Tea Garden
Mall Rd.
Happy Valley Tea Garden
Jawahar Rd. W.
Lebong Cart Rd.
Gandhi Rd
Hill Cart Rd
To Ghoom and Tiger Hill

December is the best time to come by local account, just right for snuggling up to the fire with a pot of good Darjeeling tea. The mountains are at their clearest on these crisp mornings, and the walk uphill warms the blood. But every season in Darjeeling has its appeal. September till December, after the monsoon, a temperate, amazingly green autumn spells ideal climes for trekking and the excitement of coming holidays, both Christmas and the Hindus' Dasain. Spring brings long days to enjoy picnics (also trekking) and a lively Tibetan New Year. Blossoms abound and the hotels are not yet crowded with lowlanders escaping the early summer heat.

Winding up from the hot plains of Bengal, road and railway alike slither through carpets of neatly manicured tea shrubs, rounding a final corner to greet Darjeeling. The modest town drapes itself along an aerated 2,100 m (6,890 ft) ridge and down the north-facing slope, perimeters often lost in pre-monsoon fog of early summer. Kangchendzonga rises centrestage north, flanked by Talung, Kabru, Ratong and Kumbakarna to the west and Pandim,

Simvo and Siniolchu to the east, each rising above 6,000 m (20,000 ft). In the foreground unfolds an accordion of blue ridges, tiny Sikkim. Christened the Place of the Thunderbolt (Dorje Ling) by an early Buddhist sage, Darjeeling was once part and parcel to neighbouring Sikkim until 1835 when the Chogyal deeded it to the Governor General of India "out of friendship."

Today its narrow lanes zigzag up 60 degree slopes planted with gabled Victorian bungalows and stately boarding schools; roses, poinsettias, petunias and gladioli splash colour across English gardens and lanky trees shade yawning mansions, abandoned with the death of the British Raj. The sprawling Planters' Club recalls that era of ultimate decadence, while gothic churches speak for the missionaries who came for altogether different reasons. Daily pre-dawn intonations from the downtown mosque and groups of burgundy-robed Buddhists *lamas* mingling at the vegetable mart add to the religious melting pot.

Imagine it's a crystalline winter morning, and you have had a good night's sleep tucked into a thick down comforter.

Darjeeling, A Walking City

Put on your walking shoes and join the early strollers along Chowrastha, the beginning of a full day on foot. Visit a secluded Buddhist monastery and the Tibetan Centre where handicrafts are made. After lunch spend the afternoon at the Natural History Museum or wandering through the open bazaar.

Crowning Darjeeling is **Chowrastha** pedestrian arcade and the Mall, setting the beat for a young population fond of fashion, music and Singaporean chic.

Start your tour of Chowrastha bazaar with a meal at **Glenary's** on Nehru Road, a complete bakery downstairs and an airy dining hall upstairs. From a window table you can watch pedlars setting up their stalls. On another morning, squeeze into **Dekevas** restaurant just above the **Taxi Stand** on Gandhi Road. A three course breakfast here will definitely last you through the morning.

Just above Dekevas, take note of the long verandaed **Planters' Club**, also known as the Darjeeling Club. Established in 1868, it was once the centre of social events to which tea planters rode for miles on horseback to attend weekend gatherings. To be accepted as a member of this prestigious affair was considered an honour. Women, of course, were

Tibetan women carry on traditional carpet-making

A well organised mountaineering exhibit

only allowed into a small lounge in what is now Keventer's restaurant just across the way. Open for overnight guests on temporary membership, the Club's 18 rooms, each with a fireplace, look over a spacious garden and unbeatable views of Kangchendzonga.

By 9.00 a.m., the pace on Chowrastha picks up as walking commuters scurry to work. Moving uphill from Glenary's, browse in the shops which feature a mix of souvenir clutter and attractive chunky Tibetan jewellery, strings of freshwater pearls, bells, boxes and replicas of Buddhist ritual objects along with everyday essentials such as hardware, children's toys and shoes. The **West Bengal Handicraft Development Corporation's Manjusha** emporium has a variety of handicrafts made by rural artisans under one roof; woodcarvings, appliqued pictures, woven bags, papier mache masks, bamboo knickknacks and lots more.

A worthwhile stop is **Das Studio**, 15 Nehru Road, the purveyor of postcards, film and beautiful photo enlargements of Darjeeling and the Himalaya, including popular mountain scenes of Nepal. Mr D.D. Das, the proprietor carries on a business begun in 1927 by his grandfather who moved here from Kathmandu and opened the first photography shop. He made his name producing hand colourtinted black and white enlargements and some of his collection are still on display. Besides a good photo collection of important Buddhist *lamas* of the area, Mr. Das boasts the best selection of classical Western and Hindu music cassettes.

Continuing up the pedestrian thoroughfare, you come to the **Tourist Bureau** at 1 Nehru Road, next to **Indian Airlines**. The government-run tourist information service is extremely helpful in answering questions and booking services.

In front of the Bureau the pavement stretches to a wide stage called the **Mall**. People congregate here at all times of day, resting on benches to do nothing more than people watch or grab a snack from a vendor. At one end stands a garden shrine. Ponies can be hired with or without an escort for a brisk trot down the lane. The **Oxford Book & Stationery Co.** faces the promenade, stocked with an impressive selection of books on the Himalaya.

From the Mall, follow the path to the right and signs that direct you up a short climb to **Observatory Hill**. The steps skirt the grounds of the landmark Windamere Ho-

Bhutia Bustee, an elegant village monastery

tel. Legend tells that a thunderbolt struck this high point, giving name to "Dorje Ling" and marking it sacred to both Hindus and Buddhists whose temples share the spot. You may find yourself coming back here again, at sunrise or sunset, for a view that unfolds across emerald green tea gardens down to the river, back onto the city and north toward a horizon of mountains touched with the magic of oblique sunrays.

Head around the base of Observatory Hill to the south and descend along this paved walkway, past painted *mani* stones. As the path steepens watch for signs to **Bhutia Bustee Monastery** or ask any passerby; most of Darjeeling's residents speak English and are quite used to directing outsiders along their meandering passageways. You reach the monastery in about 30 minutes from the top.

Built a century ago by the Karmapa Rinpoche, head of the

The famous Windamere Hotel.

Kargyudpa sect of Buddhism, it retains the name Bhutia in connection with its Sikkimese founder; Bustee designates it as a village monastery. Ornately decorated in red and gold, only seven *lamas* reside here year round and if one can be roused from his tasks you may go inside. Remember to send the prayer wheels spinning as you leave and then step back to capture the postcard scene on film, the Himalaya rising snow-white in the background.

The small paved path leading to the **Tibetan Refugee Self-Help Centre** strikes off from the rear left corner of the monastery, winding slightly uphill and then levelling off. Branch uphill, then within 15 minutes when in sight of the centre, head back down. Skirt several houses where directions can be sought. Looking east, you can see the oval track of the Lebong Race Course, framed in tea plantations. It is said to be the highest track in the world and races are still held during spring and autumn.

More than 700 Tibetan refugees live and work at the Centre, established in 1959 for some of the thousands who fled Tibet. Schooling and training are provided to all residents, and a remarkable handicraft production and sales unit has been built up, exporting to some 30 countries.

Visitors can walk through the workshops and observe craftsmen and women making traditional Tibetan items such as carpets, woollen boots, aprons, woodcarvings and leather goods as well as dolls, artwork, bags and clothing. The walls are plastered with posters demanding freedom for Tibet.

63

Returning to lunch in town is a pleasant 15 minute walk straight up the hill, zigzagging steeply in places through shady groves. Stay right, heading toward Jawahar Road. At the entrance to the Raj Bhawan (old royal palace grounds) turn left and navigate your way another 15 minutes back toward the **New Elgin Hotel** on H.D. Lama Road. Without marked streets it takes some exploring to hit your target the first time.

One of the nicest hotels in town, the New Elgin serves a fixed menu buffet lunch. If you prefer spicy Indian fare, try the reasonably-priced **Great Punjab Restaurant**, Robertson Road (near the Indian Bank). For a light meal, stop into **Keventer's** on Nehru Road. It is a local favourite for pint-sized hamburgers smothered in onions, and thin milk shakes.

After the monastery visit, as an alternative to walking to the Tibetan Centre, return to the Mall, grab a bite at Keventer's and a taxi at the nearby stand. Negotiate a round trip fare with waiting to the Tibetan Centre. For shopping enthusiasts, this may be preferable to carrying purchases all the way back.

In the afternoon visit the **Natural History Museum** with its exhibits of eastern Himalayan mammals, birds, reptiles, butterflies and fish, open 10 a.m. to 4 p.m. daily. It is tucked away but well marked on maps and signs are visible from the road. As an alternative, wander down to the bazaar, a labyrinth of stalls selling a mishmash of clothes, shoes, stainless steel table wear, fresh baked bread, fruits and bus tickets.

Tonight make it an early evening, with dinner at your hotel, in anticipation of a pre-dawn drive up to Tiger Hill.

Tigers Of The Mountain

Drive up to Tiger Hill for sunrise then visit monasteries before breakfast. Spend the morning in the Lloyd Botanical Garden, a tea garden and the Himalayan Mountaineering Institute. Back to town for a Tibetan lunch and a nap before a Chinese dinner and an evening stroll on the Chowrastha.

On any cloudless morning you can peek out of your hotel window and see the firelight of dawn colouring Kangchendzonga to the northeast. Everest and the Nepal peaks to the west however, are hidden from Darjeeling. For them, you must climb higher to 2,585 m (8,481 ft) on **Tiger Hill,** located 12 km (7 miles) by road from Darjeeling. There is a magnificent panoramic view of the entire eastern Himalayan range, and the very best time to see it is as the sun rises into a clear morning sky.

Soup and momos

Garden species from the world over

Fortunately, jeep taxi drivers can also be convinced to get up that early. Arrange for one at the Tourist Bureau or down at the **Taxi Stand** across from the supermarket. About US$10 will get you a round trip ride. The jeep taxi will pick you up at between 3 and 4 a.m. depending on the time of year, and transport you at the base of a short climb to the top.

It is nice to bring a thermos of hot tea or coffee to sip as the rising sun highlights the tallest peaks. The observatory platform can be packed with other anxious viewers. Along the path leading up to the top, devotees have left offerings of red *sindur* powder and miniature trident spears. Such high places hold spiritual powers that are evident to persons of all faiths.

On the way back, your driver will stop at **Senchal Lake**, a water supply reservoir in a pastoral setting. Where the Tiger Hill road joins **Hill Cart Road** at Ghoom, stop at **Samten Choling** and **Thupten Sanga Choling** monasteries now if your driver is willing to wait. Save the Yiga-Choling Monastery for another day and combine it with a ride on the Toy Train (see Itinerary 14).

You are back at your hotel by 8 a.m. in time for breakfast. Set off down the hill again past the Taxi Stand. To the right of the supermarket building watch for an unsigned road that leads down to the refreshing **Lloyd Botanic Garden.**

A five minute walk takes you away from the urban chaos to a demure hillside of azaleas and lilies, weeping willows and maples, ferns and conifers. Here young lovers go to be alone and Indian families on holiday revel in the cool "high altitude" air.

The 40 acre garden was donated in 1878 for the study of Himalayan flora by Captain William Lloyd, commander of the British frontier force at Titalia. It was he, with Governor General J.W. Grant who "discovered" Darjeeling and suggested that it would

GURU BEER

INSTANT
MOOD MAKER

Cultivating a youthful image

make an ideal health resort for ailing British troops.

The floral landscape, later supplemented with species from nearly every continent, were to be much enjoyed by British visitors who pined for their English gardens. Greenhouses nurture orchids and fragile ferns, and spacious lawns invite a picnic or snooze. The gardens are open from 8 a.m. to 6 p.m. daily except Sunday, no entry charge. Leave the way you came. Turn left down the footpath by which you left the supermarket site. This path takes you to the **Happy Valley Tea Gardens** (30 minutes walk) where you can take a tour of tea processing. The estate is closed during lunch but welcomes visitors at any other time up to 4.30 p.m. (closed on Sunday afternoons and Mondays).

There are now some 70 tea estates within the Darjeeling area, filling teapots in nearly every corner of the world. Some of the larger estates employ whole families and provide housing, schooling and health care to their employees. Along the roadside, you see women watching the babies of a dozen or so pickers, swinging the infants in slings hung from shady shelters. Darjeeling tea is free of artificial colouring or flavouring and can be purchased in town.

Skirt the hillside above the Government College (check your map) and proceed along **Lebong Cart Road** to the turn off up to Jawahar Road. At the upper intersection, turn left to the **Himalayan Zoological Park**. A small zoo, specialising in animals of the Himalaya and Central Asia, it is well worth a visit; an hour is usually sufficient. Many of the mammals and birds are endangered and found in few other zoos of the world.

The Siberian tiger only survives in zoos of South Asia and the rare snow leopard is bred here to increase its chances of survival. The Himalayan black bear, wild yak, Tibetan wolf, red panda, Royal Bengal tiger, *goral* (mountain goat) and black panther are among other threatened species kept here, their natural habitats shrinking under the encroachment of human activities. Species like the barking deer, spotted deer, other goats and antelopes, pheasant and hawks have adapted better.

Next stop is the **Himalayan Mountaineering Institute**, another unique showplace. Continue up the road beyond the zoo. Open to visitors daily 9 a.m. to 5 p.m. (to 4.30 p.m. in winter), the Institute contains two museums and a library well stocked with books on mountaineering as well as natural history of the Himalaya.

The main museum contains a relief map of the Himalaya and a climbing history of the world's highest peaks. An entire wall is covered with photographs of top mountaineers since 1760. Displays of equipment and a set-up of a typical mountaineer's tent brings the chilling scenes closer. Models wear traditional garb of peoples native to the Himalaya and upstairs is a bird and butterfly collection. Next door, the Everest museum chronicles the history of Everest since 1852 when the peak, then known merely as Peak XV, was identified as the highest in the world by a clerk under Sir George Everest, the Surveyor General of India. Surveying techniques being what they were Everest was pegged at only 8,840 m (29,002 ft), later adjusted to 8,848 m (29,028ft) as it officially stands today.

Tenzing Norgay and Sir Edmund Hillary were the first two persons to reach the summit of Mount Everest on May 29, 1953. As Director of Field Training at the Himalayan Mountaineering Institute from 1954 to 1976, Tenzing inspired and taught many young mountaineers and was active as an advisor until his death in 1986. The current Director is Nowang Gombu, first person to climb Everest twice. The Institute gives month-long basic and advanced courses in mountaineering training every spring and autumn. There is a small gift shop outside selling badges and books.

After sharing the agonies of mountaineers high on the mountain, the walk back to town is a breeze. Head toward the intersection of Chowrastha and Nehru Road, then down a few more zigzags. About half way down on the left you see the **New Dish** restaurant, popular for lunch with the locals.

All booths are curtained, a Darjeeling tradition, and here you can find some of the best *momos* and *thukpa*, a spicy Tibetan noodle and meat or vegetable soup in town. If you come too late, the day's ration of *momos* will be gone. A bottle of good Indian beer – Black Label, Dansburg, Soren – will ensure that you slip soundly into that nap. Or take in a movie at one of the cinema halls.

In the evening try **Hotel Valentino** (6 Rockville Street, tel. 2228) for good Chinese food. Right of the Telegraph office on Gandhi Road, take an uphill street which curves left, and before bearing right you see straight ahead a path to several guest houses. Valentino's is the first one. Choose between hot Sichuan or mild Cantonese dishes, or some of both. If you are up for a short stroll after dinner, venture back up Chowrastha to the Mall for some people watching.

A leisurely day of nostalgia beginning with a ride on the Toy Train to Ghoom. A short walk brings you to Yiga-Choling Monastery. Return to town by taxi and afternoon tea in the evocative Windamere Hotel. Take dinner at the polished Central Hotel.

The Toy Train is Darjeeling's mascot, a refreshing reminder that some things never change. Completed in 1882 as an extension to the Northern Bengal State Railway linking Siliguri with Calcutta, the 90 km (56 mile) track climbs nearly 2,000 m (6,500 ft) in nine hours. Few have the patience to choose the tortoise's pace when motorised hares can take the nearby road, itself built in 1839. Dedicated train buffs however enjoy an exciting ride as the blue wooden cars swing perilously close to vertical drops on more than a few mountain bends.

The ride between Darjeeling and Ghoom, 7 km (4.5 miles) with stops to let oncoming trains pass, is much more sedate but still fun. The biggest thrill is **Bastasia Loop**, one of five complete circles manoeuvred between Darjeeling and Siliguri. The daily service departs Darjeeling station at 8.25 a.m., 10.00 a.m. and 2.30 p.m., stopping in Ghoom en route to Kurseong, Siliguri, New Jalpaiguri and on

to Calcutta or New Delhi and beyond. A return train picks up passengers at Ghoom and arrives in Darjeeling at 9.55 a.m., 4.20 p.m. and 5.30 p.m. Check current timings at the stations.

There is no need for reservations if you are only going as far as Ghoom; all seats are Rs 19. To assure getting a seat, mount the·

Dhirdham Temple

ready cars, parked across the tracks from the station, 20 minutes before the departure time and buy your ticket from the conductor when he comes around. Leaving from Darjeeling, sit on the right side for the best views, and as far from the engine as possible as chunky soot tends to drop from its smoke stack. The railway station is located on Hill Cart Road, a 10 minute walk west of the supermarket. From the tracks look down on the multi-roofed **Dhirdham Temple**, patterned after Kathmandu's Pashupatinath and dedicated to Lord Shiva.

Catch the 8.25 a.m. or 10.00 a.m. train and alight at Ghoom. Walk back along the tracks and turn left on a lane to the **Yiga-Choling Monastery**, an easy 15-20 minute walk from the station. You pass by shops selling household goods and vegetables fronting on tiny houses where Tibetans live. The road leads right to the monastery.

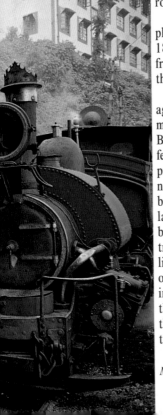

Yiga-Choling Monastery, sometimes simply called Ghoom Monastery, was built in 1850 by Lama Sharap Gyatso, a monk from Mongolia and a famous astrologist of the Gelugpa sect of Tibetan Buddhism.

The *gompa's* interior is typical of an aged Gelugpa prayer hall. At the front is a magnificent statue of Maitreya, the Future Buddha, draped in white silk scarves of offering called *katas*. Chenrezi, god of compassion, sits to the right. Tubular silk banners hang from the high ceiling and frescoes blackened by the soot of burning butter lamps cover the walls. The red and gold brocade wrapping of sacred books protrude from shelves and hand-printed pages lie unbound on low tables. Only a handful of wizened *lamas* come to chant the morning prayers. Outside, a gentle breeze stirs the long prayer flags. Walk back through the Tibetan community and hail a taxi to town on the main road.

Mascot of Darjeeling, a train buff's delight

The afternoon is yours to wander back to favourite spots or fill in what you might have missed. One "must" is the **Windamere Hotel**, a Raj landmark still considered by many as the best hotel in Darjeeling. Its guest book testifies to its advocates who return faithfully and range from dukes and mountaineers (Sir Edmund Hillary) to Tibetophiles (Heinrich Harrer), ornithologists and English grandmothers.

Take the main road left fork from the Mall and in minutes you reach its steps in a flowered embankment. The proprietor of some 50 years, the elderly Mrs. C. Tenduf-La, has almost retired but the well-spoken Mr. Sherab Tenduf-La carries on a family tradition that gives the hotel its unique ambience. Resistance to change from old friends and new fans alike is obliged by the Tenduf-Las, but service does not suffer and amenities are all you could want; those who need more have plenty of other hotels to choose from.

A private residence built in 1862, modified as a boarding house since 1889, the hotel's 27 rooms, no two alike, are tucked away in wings and cottages. A game parlour, a piano room with deep cushioned Victorian couches, a collector's library and plenty of quiet nooks encourage congeniality amongst guests. Black and white photographs illustrate the faded charms of Darjeeling's social gatherings and lend a sense of history to the untarnished *joie de vivre* of present day Darjeeling.

In a pleasant dining room off the patio, three course menus are served family style by attendants who remember not only names but favourite dishes of veteran guests. If you wish to dine at the Windamere, you must make reservations at least two hours in advance. Tea is served at any time, and you are welcome to wander the grounds. For dinner try Darjeeling's popular modern **Central Hotel** on Robertson Road, serving Indian, European and Chinese food with a panoramic view over the city and Himalaya softened by a sunset glow.

Mirik Lake Resort

A new tourist destination lies in the hills half way between Darjeeling and Siliguri. Take a day trip or stay overnight in this lovely forest setting.

The Gorkha Hill Council Tourism Department's pet project is the Mirik Lake Resort offering boating, swimming, picnics, forest walks and day treks in a cluster of cottages. Luxury coaches ply the 49 km (30 miles) from Darjeeling and regularly scheduled jeep taxis and local buses depart at 8.30 a.m. Set in a small valley, this lake-cooled enclave at 1,767 m (5,800 ft) is fast becoming a favourite with Indian tourists drawn to its water-sports and mountain view points. The drive through the countryside passes tea estates, orange

Cardamon thrives in these wet climes

groves and cardamon fields. For a holiday within a holiday, contact the Darjeeling Gorkha Hill Council, Assistant Director of Tourism, tel. (0354) 2524.

Bungalow Treks

Himalayan hikers are rediscovering Darjeeling, first trekked by Everest-bound teams of the 1920s and 1930s.
In the days when Nepal was closed to foreigners and the call of unconquered Everest pulled hard at European alpinists' heartstrings, Darjeeling was the closest trailhead. Mountaineering teams soon found themselves "trekking" through the Himalayan hill country towards base camp, unwittingly pioneering an unexpectedly important business.

Today's treks into the **Singalila Range** bordering Darjeeling and Nepal start high, at 3,636 m (12,000 ft) **Sandakphu,** from where an impressive line-up of peaks is revealed – even better than the view from Tiger Hill. Four out of five of the world's top ten mountains pierce the northern horizon; Everest (8,848 m/29,028 ft) is flanked by Lhotse (fourth highest at 8,516 m/27,940 ft), Makalu (number 5 at 8,463 m/27,766 ft) and Kangchendzonga (spelled Kangchenjunga in Nepal, third highest at 8,586 m/28,169 ft).

A seasonal jeepable road reaches Sandakphu from Darjeeling (about 55 km or 34 miles), making it accessible to the non-trekker, and a government hut provides accommodation. Eventually trekkers' alpine style huts will be in place along the entire trekking route, but for now a combination of camping in tents and sleeping in huts offers the best of both worlds.

Three to eight day treks via Sandakphu are the most popular, traversing forests of rhododendron, oak, chestnut and fir, passing lakes and village bazaars, with stunning views of the mountains

A Himalayan rain forest

from atop every ridge. The best trekking seasons are the months of March through May, and from October to December.

The Darjeeling Gorkha Hill Council is taking an active role in facilitating trekking in the area by providing guides, huts and equipment for visitors. A number of trekking agents in Darjeeling offer inclusive trek packages similar to services in Nepal and Sikkim.

No trekking permit is required.

Hikers can arrange their own treks, camping or staying with village families or in the government huts where available, though it is not advisable to trek alone anywhere in the Himalaya. It is wise to take along a guide as trails are not marked and water is not always available. Be well equipped with clothing for cold weather and follow common-sense rules of the trail; do not litter, carry out all non-burnable trash, respect dress and cultural codes of conduct, and avoid using firewood as fuel sources are scarce.

For more information, contact the Adventure Tourism Section of the Tourism Department, Darjeeling Gorkha Hill Council, Chowrastha, Darjeeling, tel. 2524.

Other adventure sports are being developed in Darjeeling and including **rafting on the Rangit River**, **fishing** for trout and larger Himalayan varieties, and even **hang-gliding**.

A Wild Time At Jaldapara

Jaldapara Wildlife Sanctuary offers a chance to see rhinos, tiger and other animals of South Asia in an easily accessible natural setting.

Compared to Tiger Tops and Nepal's Chitwan National Park, Jaldapara rings no bells of recognition among safari adventurists but that does not bother the animals who find refuge here. Established in 1941 for the protection of wildlife, particularly the Greater One-horned rhinoceros, which were losing natural habitat to the cultivation of tea at the base of the Bhutan hills, the sanctuary has enabled at least 50 rhinos to survive. Other animals living here include the Royal Bengal tiger, leopard; the sambar, swamp, barking and hog deer; wild boar, gaur and many varieties of bird including the rare Bengal florican.

The 115 sq km (44 sq mile) area, bisected by the River Torsa, supports extensive belts of tall grass and thick mixed deciduous forest, making elephant riding the only way to move about and view the animals. The best season to come is October through May, March-early April being ideal when animals graze on new grass shoots. Jaldapara is accessible from Siliguri by road (140 km, 87 miles) or train, located 7 km (4.5 miles) from the Madarihat Railway Station. Food and lodging are available at the Madarihat Tourist Lodge (West Bengal Tourism Development Corporation) or at the Hollong Forest Lodge.

Weekend package tours are the easiest way to put a visit together. The main Darjeeling Tourist Bureau at 1 Nehru Road or the Tourist Bureau, West Bengal Government at Hill Cart Road, Siliguri (tel. 21632) organises weekend excursions departing from Siliguri every Saturday morning and returning Sunday evening (during the season). The tour includes a brief visit to Phuntsholing, the lovely entryway to the Kingdom of Bhutan.

KALIMPONG

There is nothing in Kalimpong that you cannot live without seeing, yet somehow this small trading town slips irresistibly into your affections.

Without the Raj reputation of Darjeeling or the royal mystique of Sikkim, Kalimpong's charm beckons to be revealed. There is no better place to discard the hassles of harried sightseeing and soak in the natural beauty of the Himalaya.

A political hot potato tossed between neighbouring Sikkim, Bhutan, Nepal and India, Kalimpong was for the last century everybody's trophy, but more for its strategic value as a prosperous trade post than for its natural resources or its pretty face. Political climates change, but not the inherent charms which today bring international tourists to enjoy peaceful Kalimpong.

Reaching to about 1,250 m (4,100 ft) above sea level, Kalimpong straddles a northeasterly ridge flanked by two rivers, on the west the Rangit draining the Singalila range, and on the east the Relli which joins the Tista River further south.

West from Kalimpong to the north of the hills of Sikkim, is Darjeeling, higher by 1,000m (3,300 ft). Beyond, spanning the

A refreshing quaintness pervades historic Kalimpong

horizon from east to west, rise the Himalayan ramparts marking the boundaries between countries but not age-old cultures.

Kalimpong, "The Ridge Where We Play"

A day exploring central Kalimpong: Drive to the monastery viewpoint of Rinkingpong Hill, visit a nursery then enjoy momos for lunch. The handicraft centre and a local church are worth seeing before returning to your hotel for tea.

Rinkingpong Hill, locally known as **Durpin Dara**, at 1,400 m (4,650 ft) is one of two lookout points over the Kalimpong area. Its singsong name means "Binocular Ridge", being the point from which triangulations were made for the original survey of Kalimpong. It is the first stop on today's tour of central Kalimpong. Rinkingpong – the sound connotes a game of table tennis – is important in Kalimpong's history as recorded by British resident historian Dr. R. K. Sprigg. The fourth Deb Raja (King) of Bhutan deposed Kalimpong's indigenous Lepcha leader in the late 17th century and installed an administrator at a fort in Dunsong, located about 16 km (10 miles) northeast of Kalimpong. Bhutanese revenue officials came from Dunsong once a year to Rinkingpong Hill to collect grain and other produce as taxes from the Lepcha villagers. When their tax paying duties were finished, the local tribesmen would enjoy field sports on the relatively level ground. The name Kalimpong means in Lepcha "The Ridge Where We Play." Other sources give a Tibetan translation to the name, as "Hillock of Assemblage" or "Stockade of the King's Ministers."

The British took control after the Sinchula Treaty of 1865 and the community was alternately administered as an independent subdivision or as part of Darjeeling and is now absorbed in the sprawling Indian state of West Bengal, governed from Calcutta. In order to appease the 1988-1989 demands of Darjeeling and Kalimpong opposition parties for an independent state, the Gorkha Hill Council was set up to give greater authority to these hill peoples. All is now peaceful in Kalimpong and its townspeople welcome visitors with open arms.

The playing fields of Durpin Dara are now a military instalment complete with helipad, and

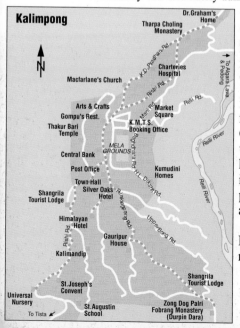

Kalimpong

Dr. Graham's Home
Tharpa Choling Monastery
K.D. Pradhan Rd.
To Algara Lava & Pedong
Charteries Hospital
Rishi Rd.
Macfarlane's Church
Men Rd.
Relli Rd.
Arts & Crafts
Market Square
Gompu's Rest.
Thakur Bari Temple
K.M.T.S. Booking Office
Rinkingpong Hill Dikshit Rd.
MELA GROUNDS
Relli River
Central Bank
Post Office
Kumudini Homes
Town Hall
Silver Oaks Hotel
Relli River
Shangrila Tourist Lodge
Rinkingpong Rd.
Himalayan Hotel
Upper Bong Rd.
Rishi Rd.
Gauripur House
Kalimandip
Shangrila Tourist Lodge
St. Joseph's Convent
Universal Nursery
St. Augustin School
Zong Dog Palri Fobrang Monastery (Durpin Dara)
To Tista

74

Object of meditation, the mandala

the **Zong Dog Palri Fobrang Monastery.** The entire south end of Kalimpong is occupied by an Indian army enclave, including a magnificent golf course (unfortunately not open to the public). Taxis are allowed to take tourists through the army compound to the monastery viewpoint but hikers may have difficulty passing the checkpost, depending upon the guard's mood.

Zong Dog Palri Fobrang was built in 1972 by the Honourable Dujen Rinpoche, whose ashes rest in a silk-encased box housed on the second of three levels. The castle-like building with brilliant golden roofs, is filled with stunning artwork. Inside over the entrance a wall of caves hold small statues of meditating *lamas*. Wall and ceiling paintings, particularly the *mandalas*, and hefty pillars are fresh with colour. The Indian scholar Padmasambhava gazes over the rich surroundings from the altar. Upstairs is a three dimensional representation of heaven, a wooden structure studded with jewels, reminiscent of Padmasambhava's celestial palace in Sikkim's Pemayangtse monastery. On the very top is a small chapel, sometimes locked, decorated with images of skeletons and a terrace with a 360 degree view of the surrounding landscape. A large field performs a dual function as exercise ground for the troops and as a forum for mass gatherings such as when His Holiness the Dalai Lama comes to visit.

Driving back into town, you pass through the prolific greenery

The wheel of dharma looks down from Durpin Dara

covering the hillside. At this middle elevation, temperatures and rainfall remain moderate with a maximum of 27°C (80.6°F) in summer and a minimum of 7.2°C (45°F) in winter. Annual rainfall tallies at 220 cm (87 ins), considerably less than Darjeeling's 320 cm (126 ins) or Gangtok's 343 cm (135 ins). The climate, and a conscious decision not to clear hillsides for tea plantations, can be credited for Kalimpong's healthy forests harbouring some 400 species of orchids, a third of the Himalayan species of rhododendron and thousands of other flowering plants.

The local horticulture industry is flourishing and 40-50 nurseries grow potted and cut flowers for domestic sale as well as export. Some of the specialities of the region are anthuriums, roses, dahlias, gladioli, gerberas, cacti and of course, the Queen of the Forest, the orchid. Some nurseries open their doors to visitors, preferably by appointment so call first from your hotel. The larger nurseries are **Universal, Standard, Twin Brothers, and Sri Ganesh Mani Pradhan and Sri L.B. Pradhan Nurseries.**

Since the 1970s, a few specialists have been hybridising and artificial propagating orchids. Native to the Kalimpong forests, orchids do well in nursery greenhouses; the major species are Dendroviums, Coekogynes, Vandas, Phalaenopsis, Cymbidiums and Bulbophyllums. Mr. Udai C. Pradhan assisted by his wife Tej, are developing new strains as well as conserving the old ones in their native habitat. To view orchids in their natural forest setting, timing is critical, and Mr. Pradhan recommends the second week in April to the first week in May as most opportune for the Kalimpong area. Some at higher reaches will be in bloom well into May and June. The trekking route is being developed from Lava to Bindu, a route chosen for its abundant floral and faunal diversity.

After the nursery visit, stop for some *momos* or Chinese fare at **Lee Restaurant** on Rishi Road, just a few minutes walk from **Gompu's Restaurant** which serves tea and snacks.

"Downtown" Kalimpong has plenty of interest to fill the afternoon. Start at the **Arts and Crafts Cooperative Centre** showroom, located down a dirt path marked by a sign near the intersection of K.D. Pradhan and Rishi Roads. Handicrafts such as bags, tablecloths, scarves, embroidered pictures and baby clothes of Lepcha, Sikkimese and Bhutanese designs produced mostly by disadvantaged women are sold here. The centre is open from 9.00 a.m. to 3.30 p.m. daily, Sundays 9.00 to 12.30 p.m.

Wander through the bazaar, heading east from the crafts centre on any

lane. Kalimpong is small enough that you can explore and never get lost; all streets lead back either to Gomphu's restaurant corner or to the Motor Stand. This old bazaar section, known locally as the **10th Mile**, is filled with shops selling Tibetan stuff, from bags and bracelets to wooden *tongba* pots and *tsampa*, a roasted flour which serves as the staple of the highland Tibetan diet. Until fifty years ago, Kalimpong was filled with Tibetans, wild men of the mountains who livened these familiar streets, chasing down their stray mules and flaunting daggers as they sparred over prices with Marwari wool buyers. On Wednesdays and Sundays, the bazaar is crowded and colourful with hill people from the surrounding areas.

The **Himalayan Hotel** still captures the romance of a turn of the century boarding house. Wood floors and stone walls convey the warm feeling of a mountain lodge, but Tibetan furnishings disclose a different history. Once the home of a leading Kalimpong British family – the author Annie Perry grew up here – the large sitting room with fireplace invites guests to gather and make use of a personal collection of Tibet literature.

Another hotel which was a former British residence is the **Singamare Tourist Lodge,** the best of three hotel undertakings of the West Bengal Tourism Development Corporation in Kalimpong. Its Tashiding Annex was once the residence of ex-Prime Minister of Bhutan, Mr. Jigme Dorje. The **Shangrila** and **Hilltop Tourist Lodges** are next in line, while the private **Kalimpong Park Hotel** is well managed and attractive. The **Hotel Silver Oaks** is more luxurious and closer to town.

High on the hill overlooking the downtown is an unexpected sight – the steeple of an unquestionably Christian church. The **Macfarlane Church** celebrated its centenary in 1991 and was founded by a Scottish pastor. Subsequent British missionaries established good schools, more churches, hospitals and a resolute Christian congregation. Other chapels of this Himalayan community show a character of their own; the religious wall paintings of **St. Augustine's School** have a distinctively Tibetan visage, while the **Sister of Charity's** chapel is more a Tibetan monastic building with murals showing what appear to be scenes from the Bible enacted by Tibetans. St. Augustine's School is located to the south of town and could be combined with a visit to the Universal Nursery.

By now its probably time to head back to your hotel. If you want to go into town for dinner, plan an early evening as taxis can be hard to find after 8.00 p.m.

A Home With A View

The famous Dr. Graham's Home stop Deolo Hill provides an excellent vantage on the Himalaya. Walk or drive up, take a picnic and enjoy a solitary afternoon. On the way stop in at two important monasteries.

Dr. Graham's Home is a Kalimpong landmark. Founded in 1900 by Scotsman, Rev. Dr. John Anderson Graham as a home for six orphans, it is now a school for 900 students and has inspired the establishment of other homes for the handicapped and destitute throughout Kalimpong.

A hike up to the site is a pleasant way to spend the morning. From the main bazaar, make your way to the Macfarlane Church and head northeast (right) along K. D. Pradhan Road on past the Hospital. Within 30 minutes you reach **Tharpa Choling Monastery,** built in 1937 with donations from the hundreds of Tibetans traders who showed their gratitude for safely crossing the Himalaya with generous offerings to the gods.

From here following the ridge reaching **Dr. Graham's Home** and continue on up to **Deolo Hilltop** (1,700 m, 5,590 ft), passing the city's reservoir **Deolo Lake**. Water is carried here by pipe from springs some 30 km (19 miles) away.

From this high point, you can look straight down nearly 1.6 km (1 mile) to the confluence of the Tista and Rangit Rivers, noticing their contrasting colours.

On the return, trace your way back to the monastery and take the lower road. Close to town, you see below the oldest monastery in Kalimpong **Thongsa Monastery,** circa 1692, built in the Bhutanese. A line of willowy eucalyptus trees circle its compound. You are welcome to visit the lower and upper prayer rooms. Continue back to town via the 10th Mile Tibetan shops.

Shopping

Shopping for souvenirs is made easy in Gangtok, Darjeeling and Kalimpong by the concentration of shops in and around **M.G. Marg, Chowrastha** and **Rishi Road**. At cottage industry centres you can see handicrafts being made and select from a variety of items under one roof. Bargaining is expected – try to establish a fair price, recognising the hours that went into an item – except in training centres where profits benefit the disadvantaged.

Woodcarvings and Tibetan Carpets

The Sikkimese *choktse,* an ornately carved, foldable wooden table stained naturally or brightly painted, makes a memorable although bulky souvenir. The **Government Institute of Cottage Industries** in Gangtok (sales room open daily 9:30-4:00) sells them for US$30-50.

Tibetan-style woolen carpets and seat coverings (1mx2m or 3ftx6ft and 50cm-60cm or 20-24in square) are made of thick sheep wool. Dyed with vegetable and mineral estracts (some chemical too) they are knotted into traditional) designs and Buddhist symbols and sold (price range: US$50-100) at the Government Institute, the **Sikkim Rural Development Showroom** (at the junction M. G. Marg and the New Market) and at the **West Bengal Handicraft Development Corporation** (Chowrastha, Darjeeling).

Cloth Apparel and Weaving

Often confused with Bhutanese weaving, the Lepcha style hand-loom cloth is sewn into bags, bed covers, curtains, table mats, cushion covers and belts, and sold throughout the region.

Sikkimese garments such as the *kho* and *honju* can be purchased ready-made or custom tailored at Gangtok's **Lhasa Tailor**, located near the upper Taxi Stand. The striped apron (*pangden*) is sold ready-made or in lengths in any Tibetan shop, and are seen on the loom at the **Tibetan Refugee Self-Help Centre** in Darjeeling or in shops along **10th mile** bazaar in Kalimpong. The Kalimpong **Arts**

and Crafts Cooperative Centre sells various cloth items as well.

Hand-knit sweaters and homespun fabrics are reasonably priced at the Sikkim Rural Development Showroom. Inexpensive applique pictures of Sikkimese and Tibetan scenes are seen in gift shops everywhere. Colourful felt and leather Tibetan boots are sewn at Darjeeling's Tibetan refugee centre, and lively Kathmandu-style clothes are finding their way into Darjeeling's Chowrastha shops.

Jewellery, *Thangkas* and Antiques

Copper, brass and silver (or "white metal") bracelets, ethnic design necklaces, and earrings are made for tourists and moderately priced. The more authentic turquoise, coral and zee-stone necklaces worn by the Sikkimese arepriced considerably higher. Fresh water pearl are popular in Darjeeling.

Originally used by travelling *lamas* as objects of meditation and teaching, the *thangka* is also a highly developed art form. Delicately stroked figures, some highlighted in gold are a measure of quality. Arts and crafts shops in Gangtok and Darjeeling sell *thangkas*, old and new.

Bhutia women spin prayer wheels wearing the traditional kho and pangden

Souvenir shops sell actual and imitation relics of Tibetan Buddhist heritage including wooden masks, metal *dorjes* and bells. Remember that items (more than 100 years old cannot be exported from India (see Customs).

Tea and Whiskey

To the tea connoisseur, no gift can beat a packet of fresh Sikkimese or Darjeeling tea for about Rs70-80 for 250 grams. In Sikkim, **Temi** and **Solja** brand teas are the highest grades, and **Kangchendzonga** next best. Darjeeling's labels are too numerous to list.

Sikkimese liquors hold their own against European whiskies and brandies. Shangrila Whiskey and Fireball Special Brandy are among the favourite brands, sold for about Rs50-Rs60.

Books, Film and Other Essentials

Oxford Book & Stationery Company in Darjeeling, **Jainco, General Stores,** and **K.N. Dewan Books and Periodicals** in Gangtok) carry a good selection of travel literature and periodicals. **Maps** are available at these book stores and at Tourist Information Centres.

Photo shops generally have Japanese and Indian print film, slide film is harder to come by. **Das Studio** of Darjeeling carries the best supply of film, camera accessories and offers professional processing. One hour colour processing is readily available. **Tse Ten Tashi & Co.** on M.G. Marg, Gangtok specialises in old photographs.

Travellers' sundry needs, particularly toiletries and trekking foods, can be readily found but not trekking equipment and clothes.

Sikkimese And Tibetan Cuisine

Sikkimese food incorporates flavours and ingredients from Tibet, Bhutan, Nepal and India. *Dal bhaat tarkari* (lentils, rice and meat and/or vegetable curry) flavoured with chili, cumin, turmeric, ginger and forest herbs, is the daily fare. Along with chicken and pork, beef is eaten widely unlike elsewhere in India and Nepal where cows are protected by Hindu custom.

Unfortunately, few of the restaurants in Gangtok serve true Sikkimese food on the regular menu, but at some of the larger hotels a special traditional Sikkimese dinner can be ordered in advance. Tibetan foods such as *momos* (meat stuffed steamed dumplings), *thukpa* (noodle soup with vegetables or meat), and *shabalay* (a fried meat pasty) are available at Tibetan speciality restaurants. Chinese and Indian food are also widespread and Western style foods are served at a few hotels in Darjeeling.

Family in Muguthang

There is little in the way of **evening entertainment** in any of these three hillside communities but many hotels have comfortable bars where friends gather. Some of the hotels offer **cultural programmes** on advance request, also arranged through Sikkim Tourism or the Darjeeling Tourist Bureau.

Restaurants In Gangtok

(See Accommodations listing for hotel restaurants)

Blue Sheep, M.G. Marg. Featuring Sikkimese-Tibetan and Chinese dishes and *gyakho*, a festive group soup meal, with prior notice.

Dyzom Bar and Restaurant, Mahatma Gandhi (M.G.) Marg. A favourite among Gangtok's *momo* fans, serving Tibetan and Chinese food and drink.

Green Hotel, M.G. Marg. Tel: 3354, 2876. Serving "4-5,000 *momos* a day." Once a watering hole for visiting Tibetan nobility, set in a classic wooden hotel.

House of Bamboo, M.G. Marg. Good *thukpa* and *momos*, and other Tibetan and Chinese specialities. Mix here with Gangtok's young set in a soft rock atmosphere.

Porky's, at the Dolph Inn, Deorali (near the Institute of Tibetology), Tel: 3032, 2231. Serving from an extensive Chinese, Continental and Indian menu, with juicy pork *momos*. Bar and bakery attached.

Sanvinak Restaurant and Bar, M.G. Marg. Offering light meals of sandwiches, burgers, Chinese and Indian dishes. Hard liquor available evenings.

Restaurants In Darjeeling

Dekevas, Gandhi Road. A great one dollar three-course breakfast, plus sandwiches, burgers, pizza, etc.

Great Punjab Restaurant, Robertson Road. An inelegant but decent Indian restaurant, tandoori, curries, biryani, nan, vegetarian and non-vegetarian.

Glenary's, Nehru Road. Above an aromatic bakery, serving breakfasts and other Western selections, plus ice cream.

Keventer's, Nehru Road. A popular corner burger and malt stop. Tiny burgers and thin malts, order double.

New Dish, N.B. Singh Road. A boothed restaurant, specialising in *momos*, meat dishes and drinks for an after-work crowd.

Restaurants In Kalimpong

Lee Restaurant, Rishi Road, Tel: 333. Serving *momos*, Cantonese and Tibetan food, close to the central bazaar.

Gompu's Hotel, Damber Chowk (Main Road). Popular for tea, sweets and snacks, with attached bar and some rooms.

Calendar of Special Events

Festivals are times to please and appease the gods with demonstrations of devotion, to give thanks for demonstrated favour and to inspire the success of good over evil. On auspicious dates set each year by the lunar calendar, Buddhists gather at major monasteries to witness *lamas*, portrayed as the deities themselves, act out dance-dramas illustrating the ultimate triumph of the virtuous.

Hindus worship their own deities, among a pantheon of three million, and on festival days bath in sacred waters or sacrifice animals to their supreme goddess. As dates vary from year to year, the times given are only approximate. Final dates can only be known with the publication of the New Year's calendar so check with the Sikkim and Darjeeling Tourist Offices.

Visitors are welcome to join in these celebrations, remembering that performances are actual blessings or exorcisms which hold providential significance for the people. Always inquire if photography is allowed and take pictures with utmost discretion.

Sikkim Festival Calendar

December-January

Kagyat Dance (28th & 29th day of 10th Tibetan month). Two days prior to Lossong, the Sikkimese New Year, dances are held in several monasteries including Tsuklakhang. Effigies are burned representing destruction of evil, inviting an auspicious new year.

Lossong (usually in December). Also called Sonom Losar (or Farmers' New Year), the Sikkimese celebrate the harvest with family gatherings, special foods and archery contests.

Enchey Chaam (18th & 19th days

Black Hat dance at Rumtek

of the 11th Tibetan month). As at each major monastery at different times of year, the *lamas* at Enchey Monastery perform ritual dances wearing elaborate silk costumes and terrifying masks.

Magha Sankranti (1st day of Nepali month Magha). On this day Hindus ritually bathe at a holy spot, commemorating the passing of cruel winter and welcoming the spring.

February-March

Guthor (Winter) Chaam (two days prior to Losar). *Chaam* dances held at Rumtek and Pemayangtse monasteries usher in the Tibetan New Year, wiping the previous year's slate clean to start anew.

Losar (Tibetan New Year, first day of the Tibetan year). Celebrated for several days before and after the first at monasteries as well as homes (government offices are closed).

Tashiding Bumchu (15th day of the 1st Tibetan month). Sikkimese gather at Tashiding monastery to receive the blessing of the Bumchu, sacred water which has been kept in a vessel for 300 years and never runs dry.

April-May

Flower Festival (March through May). Calling international attention to Sikkim's rich floral resources, tour packages arranged by the Department of Tourism visit the major monasteries and gardens; a flower show is held at the White Hall in Gangtok.

May-June

Saga Dawa (15th day, full moon, of the 4th Tibetan month). Also known as Duechen Sumzom (Triple Blessing), on this day 2,500 years ago Buddha's soul entered his mother's womb; as an adult, he both attained

enlightenment and later passed onto *nirvana* on this day. A procession wends through Gangtok and other communities.

Tse Chu Chaam (10th day of the fifth Tibetan month). At Rumtek monastery, a great dance drama is performed by costumed *lamas*, depicting the life of Guru Rinpoche or Padmasambhava, the Indian sage who spread Buddhism throughout Tibet.

Giving New Year's blessings at Rumtek

July-August-September

Drukpa Tseshi (4th day of the 6th Tibetan month). Commemorating Buddha's first teaching (the Turning of the Wheel of Dharma), this day is marked by worship at Phurba Chorten in Gangtok.

Pang Lhabsol (15th day of the 7th Tibetan month). Performed only in Sikkim in honour of the guardian deities Kangchendzonga and Yabdu. Dancers wearing warrior-like costumes perform in front of the Tsulkakhang.

October-November

Dasain & Diwali (during the Hindu months Ashwin and Kartik). During 10 days of Dasain devotees pay homage to supreme goddess Durga with blood sacrifices of male chickens, goats and buffalo. Family members receive a *tika* (a red powder blessing mark on the forehead). Three weeks later, **Diwali** (or Tihar), the Festival of Lights takes place, inviting Lakshmi, Goddess of Wealth, to enter every Hindu home.

Darjeeling And Kalimpong Festivals And National Holidays

Besides **Losar** (Tibetan New Year), mostly Hindu and Christian festivals are celebrated in Darjeeling and Kalimpong. **Holi** (in March) is a raucous time when coloured powders and water are thrown over passersby.

Gandhi Jayanti (Mahatma Gandhi's birthday) is October 2. Republic Day (January 26) and **Independence Day** (August 15) are National Holidays throughout India. Christian holidays Christmas, New Years Day, Good Friday and several Islamic holy days are marked by government holidays as well.

Darjeeling and Kalimpong usually stage **Tourist Festivals** each year as well, featuring cultural dances and special events. In **Pedong**, a small town located to the northeast from Kalimpong, an annual week-long mela is held at the end of February.

Distributing Bumchu at Tashiding

Practical Information

GETTING THERE

By Air

There is no direct air service to Sikkim, Darjeeling nor Kalimpong. The closest airport is at Bagdogra, 124km (77 miles) and about five hours drive from Gangtok, four hours from Darjeeling and three from Kalimpong.

Indian Airlines departs Delhi on Tuesdays, Thursdays and Saturdays at 6.30am and arrives in Bagdogra at 8.20am, returning at 2.10pm arriving in Delhi at 4.15pm. The fare is US$128 one way.

Except for Mondays, a daily flight departs Calcutta at 11am and arrives in Bagdogra at 11.55am; Mondays at 1.30pm, arriving at 2.15pm. Return flights depart Bagdogra daily except Mondays at 12.25pm arriving at 1.20pm; Monday at 2.45pm arriving at 3.40pm. The one way fare is US$50.

As schedules and fares change frequently, please check with the airlines for current information. Indian Airlines offices in Gangtok, Darjeeling and Kalimpong (see Addresses below) can book and confirm domestic flights only. Confirm all tickets three days in advance.

By Rail

Rail service connects Delhi with Siliguri (for Sikkim and Kalimpong) and New Jalpaiguri (for Darjeeling). The "Toy Train" plies between Darjeeling and New Jalpaiguri several times daily. Long distance trains also run daily between Siliguri and Calcutta, Lucknow and other major Indian cities.

By Road

Buses: Sikkim Nationalised Transport (SNT) provides daily services between Siliguri and Gangtok, with a daily direct bus to the Bagdogra airport (departing Gangtok at 7am). Passengers arriving in Bagdogra airport can take a taxi or rickshaw to the SNT bus station in Siliguri. Private buses run throughout the day.

The Darjeeling Tourist Bureau and Indian Airlines in Kalimpong also operate daily buses to the airport, connecting to Delhi or Calcutta-bound flights.

Taxis: Taxi vans, jeeps or sedans (usually Indian-made Ambassadors or Maruti cars) can be hired from Siliguri to Gangtok (about Rs800), to Darjeeling (Rs600) or Kalimpong (Rs400). Taxis wait near the Nepal border crossing, or can be arranged at a hotel in Siliguri, near the bus or rail station or airport.

To and From Nepal and Bhutan

There are no direct flights between Kathmandu and Bagdogra; the only Indian Airlines connection is via Delhi or Calcutta. Otherwise, fly from Kathmandu to Biratnagar (daily flights on Royal Nepal Airlines, US$77) and drive from there. You can catch a bus or a taxi from Biratnagar to Kakarbhitta (three hours, taxi charge about the equivalent of US$30-$40) and after passing through Immigration Checkposts on both the Nepal and India sides, arrange transport onward (see above). When departing India, take a bus or taxi from Kakarbhitta to Biratnagar and fly to Kathmandu. Be sure to confirm your flight the day before.

The alternative is to take the night bus to or from Kathmandu to Kakarbhitta, a 15-hour journey under less than idyllic conditions costing less than US$5. Book seats in advance in Kathmandu; seats are plentiful departing from Kakarbhitta.

From Bhutan, drive from Phuntsholing at the west Bhutan border to the Tista River (about three hours) where you join the road to Sikkim or Darjeeling.

TRAVEL ESSENTIALS

When to Visit

Except for the monsoon months from mid-June to mid-September, any time of year is enjoyable at these temperate latitudes. During monsoon, travel can be hampered due to road wash-outs; walking through the countryside is dubious with abundant leeches and the mountains are often veiled in persistent drizzle. July and August tend to see more rain than June.

Autumn has always been touted as the best time to visit the Himalaya for clear skies and harvest colour. Trekking is primo from October to mid-December. The temperature in Gangtok drops to 5°C (41°F) through mid-January, slightly warmer in Kalimpong and Darjeeling.

Spring comes early, often by mid-February and a season to herald it is. Beginning at middle elevations, the rhododendrons burst forth by mid-March, moving up the hillsides to 3,500m (12,000ft) by mid-May. Orchids likewise open up as slopes warm from low to high, peaking in April and May.

Visas and Permits

Besides a valid passport (good for the duration of your stay) and an Indian visa, there are no special permit requirements for Darjeeling nor Kalimpong. You cannot extend your Indian visa in Darjeeling, Kalimpong or Sikkim.

It is advisable to get your Indian visa in your own home country.

A special permit is required to visit Sikkim. A tourist may stay up to 15 days and the permit can be issued within an hour by Sikkim Tourism offices in Siliguri (closed Sundays and government holidays), at the Foreigner Registration Office (FRO) in Darjeeling or at airports in Calcutta or Delhi. A Sikkim permit can also be issued on a valid Indian visa at any Indian mission abroad.

A checkpost at Tista checks Darjeeling and Kalimpong bound travellers. Another checkpost before Rangpo and one inside the Rangpo Tourist Lodge just over the border ask for your Sikkim permit. Other entry points to Sikkim are Melli and Rammam Bridge near Jorethang.

Tourists travelling outside of Gangtok must have authorization permitting travel to Pemayangtse, Phodang and Rumtek. Such permission can be obtained at the time of application or from the Tourist Information Centre in Gangtok. A checkpost at Geyzing and Legship (West Sikkim) inspects foreigners' permits. Only those with a trekking permit may visit Tashiding Monastery.

Trekking Permits: In Sikkim, foreigners must trek in a group of at least four and contract with a registered trekking agent. Indian nationals can trek unaccompanied and need no permit. It takes one day to process a trekking permit, through an agent in Gangtok or Darjeeling. One photo is required and there is no fee. Trekking permits must be shown at Yuksom. No trekking permit is needed in Darjeeling or Kalimpong.

Mountaineering Permit: Mountaineering expeditions must apply to the Indian Mountaineering Foundation (IMF) for a permit to climb any peak. Peaks consid-

Clothing

In the City: Except for special occasions, dress is informal. Around town and especially at the monasteries, women should avoid wearing shorts and skimpy tops; likewise, men should wear full pants and shirts with sleeves at monasteries. Bring a warm sweater or jacket for mornings and evenings throughout winter and early spring. An umbrella offers the best protection from monsoon rains and bring shoes that can tolerate soggy conditions.

ered sacred to the Sikkimese are normally not open to foreigners. These include Mounts Kangchendzonga, Narsingh, Kabru North and South, Kabru Dome, Pandim, Goecha, Forked Peak and Pao Hungri. For permission to climb lower peaks (5,800m, 19,000ft) applications can be made directly to Sikkim Tourism, Adventure Section or to the DGHC, Tourism Department, Darjeeling.

Vaccinations

There are no required inoculations for Sikkim, Darjeeling or Kalimpong. Visitors arriving in India from countries infected by yellow fever must show a certificate of valid yellow fever inoculation. By personal choice, inoculations against typhoid, hepatitis (gamma globulin), tetanus, polio and meningitis are recommended.

Customs

There are no customs regulations specific to Sikkim, Darjeeling and Kalimpong. Indian customs regulations apply.

Professional equipment and high-value articles such as television equipment and a personal video recorder must be declared on arrival in India and a TBRE (Tourist Baggage Re-Export) form filled out. You must show articles listed and the TBRE form upon departure; duty will be charged on any items left behind.

The export of antiques (over 100 years old), animal species or products covered by the CITES convention is not permitted.

On Trek: Women trekkers will find that a below-the-knee length skirt or loose hiking pants are comfortable and in line with cultural norms. Men might wear Bermuda-length hiking shorts or pants, and always a shirt (tank tops are okay on the trail only). Good sturdy hiking shoes or boots prevent ankle twisters, and again an umbrella is your best cover in both the rain and in hot sun; otherwise a hat, sun glasses and sun screen are vital in the late spring, early fall bright sun and if approaching glaciers with their extreme reflectivity.

Electricity and Water

Throughout India, 220-v/50 cycles is used. Electricity is available in all hotels, even some Trekkers Huts, in Sikkim, Darjeeling and Kalimpong. Power outages are common even in urban areas.

Darjeeling and Kalimpong have seasonal water shortages so try to conserve.

Time Differences

Indian Standard Time extends throughout the country. It is 5-1/2 hours ahead of Greenwich Mean Time, 9-1/2 hours ahead of US Eastern Standard Time, and 15 minutes behind Nepal time.

GETTING ACQUAINTED

Cultural Sensitivity

Whereas Darjeeling and Kalimpong have acclimated to some extent to the habits and behaviour of outsiders, the Sikkimese people, especially those in the countryside and monasteries, are less familiar with the ways of foreigners. Please respect their cultures by following these tips on cultural sensitivity:

Begging and Donations: Do not encourage children's begging by giving out sweets or trinkets; instead give donations to schools or monasteries for their dispersal. It is customary to give a few rupees or some food to religious mendicants or to those who cannot work because of disability, and to leave small donations at monasteries.

Sacred Places: Respect all sacred places, from monastery grounds to sites around prayer flags or *puja* rocks and trees.

Do not litter or use such area as a toilet. Avoid stepping or climbing on holy objects. Use all four fingers of the right hand rather than a single finger when pointing to holy sites or people. Try not to touch others or sacred objects with your feet, and do not point your feet at a person, shrine or a cooking fire.

Photography: Most people do not mind having their picture taken, but some older people and others embarrassed by their dress or unfamiliar with a camera may take offence. Always ask permission before taking pictures of people, temples, statues and stupas, monks and *lamas*.

Gestures: The Indian greeting of *Namaste*, formally said with palms together in front of the chest, is a polite greeting to people of all faiths. The Tibetans and Bhutias say Tashi Delek, wishing well on thox greeted. Do not hand or receive anything with your left hand, considered "polluted"; better use two hands if possible to show appreciation. Unless you are left-handed, avoid eating among Hindus with your left hand and do not eat out of common serving dishes or expect others to share food which you have touched.

Mountain Manners: Please follow the published trekking rules: camp only in designated spots, keep campsites clean, carry out non-burnables and non-biodegradables, do not litter, do not use firewood but cook with kerosene only, respect sacred places, avoid making loud noises, and do not take undue risks.

MONEY MATTERS

Currency

The Indian rupee (IC stands for Indian currency, Rs for rupees) is divided into 100 paise. Coins are in denominations of 1, 5, 10, 25 and 50 paise. Notes are in 1, 2, 3, 5, 10, 20, 50, 100 and 500.

Exchange rates fluctuate, however at present is Rs25.55 is equivalent to one US dollar.

Major foreign currencies and travellers cheques can be changed at only those banks, hotels and money changers licensed to deal in foreign currency. It is difficult to change money outside of the cities of Gangtok, Darjeeling or Kalimpong. None of the banks in Kalimpong are licensed for foreign exchange, however some hotels can take payment in travellers cheques.

You can exchange Indian rupees back into foreign currency upon departure from India, but not to exceed the total amount originally changed. Keep all money exchange receipts to support your re-exchange. Payment for airlines tickets must be made in foreign currency. Hotel bills and travel services can be paid in rupees as long as you can show official exchange receipts for the amount.

Credit Cards

Major international credit cards and Indian credit cards are accepted in the larger hotels and a few shops in the cities. It is better to come prepared with adequate cash however to avoid problems.

Banks

Banks are generally open from 10am to 2pm Monday through Friday, 10am to noon on Saturdays, closed Sundays and government holidays. Grindlays Bank in Darjeeling is the only bank in this area that can receive immediate telexed money transfers from overseas banks. It can give payment in rupees or travellers cheques (with special instructions from the sending bank). The State Bank of India can receive telexed money transfers via its central bank, taking up to several days.

Tipping

It is customary to tip about 10 percent in better restaurants, and a few rupees to bell boys or hotel service staff. You need not tip city taxi drivers unless you ask them to wait; tipping of long distance taxi or excursion bus drivers is appreciated. Generally, travel and trekking guides receive a greater tip (equivalent to a few dollars per person per day), and cooks, porters and camp staff receive less, scaled to their responsibility and performance.

Airport Tax

There is no domestic airport tax. A tax of Rs150 must be paid upon check-in for your international departure flight.

GETTING AROUND

Buses

Sikkim Nationalised Transport (SNT) operates daily bus services between Gangtok and Darjeeling and Kalimpong. Advance bookings can be made at the SNT office in Gangtok between 9am and 12pm and 1pm and 3.30pm.

Private bus services also connect the three hill stations. SNT operates daily local buses between Gangtok and Geyzing via Rabongla, Rumtek, Namchi, Mangan, Rongli, Jorethang and Kewzing. Check at SNT office for schedule. As well, luxury coaches, cars and jeeps are available for hire at the Sikkim Tourist Information Centre, Gangtok.

The **North Bengal State Transport Corporation** operates buses service out of Darjeeling (booking and departing at the lower Taxi Stand) connecting to Siliguri and Kalimpong several times a day. Agents in Darjeeling book seats for long distance buses to Siliguri, Calcutta, Varanasi, Patna and Kathmandu. Bus-train bookings throughout India can be made as well.

Taxis and Jeeps

Group jeep taxis run more frequently than buses between major destinations. Unless you book the entire vehicle expect to be squeezed in; try for the front seat.

In and around Gangtok, car taxis do not operate on metres, rates points are posted on the windshield. Most in-city fares run Rs10-Rs30. Maruti cars, vans or jeeps can be hired for day or longer excursions. Some rates for long distances are set, others are negotiable, and a waiting or overnight charge should be paid.

There are very few individual taxis operating in and around Darjeeling. Jeep group taxis can be caught at the upper and lower Taxi Stands, or hailed along the roads coming into town.

Individual taxis can be hired in Kalimpong for around town or excursions into the countryside for a negotiated rate (check at your hotel for a reasonable charge). The Kalimpong Syndicate (at the main Taxi Stand) runs group jeep taxis to Gangtok and Darjeeling.

Sightseeing Tours

Sikkim Tourism operates daily sightseeing tours around Gangtok and to more distant sites. Morning (10am to noon) city bus tours run Rs25 person with a guide. Similarly, Darjeeling's Tourist Bureau offers scheduled sightseeing tours and excursions.

Bicycle Touring

Mountain biking is another way to tour these areas, but only for those in top fitness. Roads are incredibly steep, ascending and descending thousands of metres between destinations. Traffic is light however and unpaved roads offer some pleasant alternatives. Check with the Tourism offices as to which roads are best and where accommodations are available.

HOURS AND HOLIDAYS

In Sikkim, Darjeeling and Kalimpong, government office hours are generally open 10am to 4pm and half-days on Saturdays (9am to 1pm), closed all day Sundays. In Sikkim government offices work all day Saturdays except the second Saturday of the month; closed Sundays. Public holidays coincide with festival days.

Shops are usually open from 10am to 7pm. Most are closed Sundays.

Sunday is the big bazaar day in Gangtok, when farmers and traders sell their goods at Lall Bazaar. The main bazaar of Kalimpong is held on Wednesdays and

Saturdays, and on Sundays in Darjeeling at the bazaar near the lower Taxi Stand.

ACCOMMODATION

SIKKIM

Best Available

Hotel Mayur, Paljor Stadium Road. , Tel: 2752, 2825. 25 rooms: US$33 (sng) US$41 (dbl). An undertaking of Sikkim

Tourism, with full services, central, mediocre rooms. **Shepi Restaurant**, serving Chinese, Indian and Sikkimese dishes, with Tandoori and *gyakho* specialities.

Hotel Norkhill, Paljor Stadium Road. Tel: 3187, 3187. 26 rooms/suites: US$31 (sng) US$45 (dbl) American Plan. Where most foreign groups stay, with spacious gardens and a grand view. Built as the Chogyal's guesthouse. In-house restaurant serving Sikkimese menu and cultural show on request.

Hotel Tashi Delek, M.G. Marg. Tel: 2038, 2991, 2362. 50 rooms/suites: US$28 (sng) US$43 (dbl) American Plan. Popular with Indian tourists, a slightly aged Gangtok establishment with a scenic terrace. **Blue Poppy Restaurant and Yak Bar,** offering Tandoori Indian and a variety of other cuisines.

Hotel Tibet, Paljor Stadium Road. Tel: 2523, 3468. 30 rooms/suites: US$12 (sng) US$16 (dbl) Comfortable rooms, authentic Tibetan architecture, with books on Tibet and the office of the Dalai Lama. **Snow Lion Restaurant.** Dine on tasty Tibetan, Indian and Chinese food amidst elegant Tibetan decor.

Moderate Priced

Dolph Inn, Deorali, Tel: 3032, 2231. 11 rooms: US$10. Close to the Institute of Tibetology.

Green Hotel, M.G. Marg, Tel: 3354. 45 rooms: US$12. A Turkish-Tibetan family affair, with memorabilia and friendly folks.

Siniolchu Lodge, (near Enchey Monastery), Tel: 2074. 27 rooms: US$5 (sng) US$6 (dbl). Under Sikkim Tourism, this ridgetop location offers unparalleled views of Gangtok and Kangchendzonga.

Outside Gangtok

Hotel Kunga Deleg, Rumtek, 4 rooms: Rs50. Managed by the Dharma Chakra Centre of Rumtek monastery, offering a peaceful retreat next to the *gompa*.

Hotel Mount Pandim, Pemayangtse, Tel: 03593-256. 25 rooms/suites: US$15-$22 (sng) US$21-$27 (dbl) American Plan. Sikkim Tourism operates the only deluxe hotel outside of Gangtok. Set at 2,076m (6,800ft), the hilltop setting offers glorious views of the Himalaya.

Rangpo Tourist Lodge, Rangpo (at border crossing to Sikkim). 8 rooms: US$7-$10 (non AC/AC, single or double). A clean, new Sikkim Tourism hotel overlooking the Tista River.

Trekkers Huts, located along the trek routes and at Kechepari Lake, Pemayangtse, Tashiding, Yuksom, and Varsey. Dormitory rooms: Rs25 per bed

DARJEELING

Best Available

Central Hotel, Robertson Road., Tel: 2033, 2746. 52 rooms: US$28 (sng) US$47 (dbl) American Plan. Minutes from Chowrastha, indeed central. Full dining and hotel services.

Hotel Sinclairs Darjeeling, 18/1 Gandhi Road., Tel: 3431, 3432. 54 rooms: US$32 (sng) US$50 (dbl) American Plan. In a quiet residential neighbourhood, with sun-deck viewing onto the Kangchendzonga range.

Hotel Valentino, 6 Rockville Road. (above Telephone Exchange), Tel: 2228. 14 rooms: US$28 European Plan. An excellent Chinese restaurant attached to a modern hotel.

New Elgin Hotel, H.D. Lama Road., Tel: 3314, 3316. 25 rooms: US$31 (sng) US$46 (dbl) American Plan. A charming Victorian style hotel set amidst an English garden — 50 years ago the guesthouse of a maharaja. Some rooms with fireplace.

Planters Club, Gandhi Road., Tel: 3260. 18 rooms: US$24-$33 (dbl). For the "club-minded", recalling days of the British Raj. With a billiards room, a bar and gardens.

Windamere, Observatory Hill. Tel: 2841, 2397; Fax: 91-354-2739. 27 rooms/suites: US$50 (sng) US$80 (dbl) American Plan. A classic hotel extraordinaire, no two rooms are alike, all with fireplaces. Guests gather in historic sitting rooms and a bar that has hosted kings, mountain heros and Tibetan traders.

Moderate Priced

Hotel Tshering Denzongpa, 6 J.P. Sharma Road. Tel: 3412. 8 rooms: US$10-$21 (double). New hotel in the old bazaar. Great mountain views, no restaurant.

New Everest Hotel, 5/2 Gandhi Road. Tel: 2252. US$7-$10. An old Tibetan home pleasant, but noisy. Meals available.

Tourist Lodge, The Mall, Tel: 2611, 2612, 2613. 17 rooms/suites: US$21-$33 (double/triple) Modified American Plan A West Bengal Tourism Development Corp. venture, somewhat institutional feeling. A **Youth Hostel** (Dr. Zakir Hussain Road) is also available.

Outside Darjeeling

Mirik Tourist Lodge & Cottages, Darjeeling Gorkha Hill Council Tourism (DGHC), Tel: 37. 84 beds: US$12-$15 (dbl) US$1 (dorm). The government run tourist lodge at lakeside resort Mirik. Other private lodges are available as well.

Trekkers Huts at Sandakphu, and on trek routes. Department of Tourism, DGHC, Tourist Bureau, Chowrastha, Darjeeling, Tel: 2524

KALIMPONG

Best Available

Hotel Silver Oaks, Rinkingpong Road, Tel: 296, 368, 766, 767. 25 rooms: US$31 (sng) US$46 (dbl) American Plan. Deluxe rooms, close to town with pleasant gardens looking on mountain.

Kalimpong Park Hotel, Rinkingpong Road, Tel: 304. US$12-$19 (sng) US$15-

$31 (dbl) European/American Plan. Pleasant, clean garden hotel with friendly staff, good food. Once the summer home of a maharaja.

Kalimpong (Singamare) Tourist Lodge and Tashiding Annex, Rinkingpong Road, Tel: 384. 13 rooms (with annex): US$8 (single) US$15-$26 (double). A charming hotel, once the George Morgan residence, with extensive gardens, singular rooms some with fireplace. A WBTDC venture.

Himalayan Hotel, Tel: 248. 11 rooms: US$12 (sng) US$16 (dbl) Bed & Breakfast
A classic lodge cum home, hosting early Tibet travellers, it still retains an aura of romance and warmth. Tibetan memorabilia and library.

Moderate Priced

Shangrila Tourist Lodge (WBTDC), Tel: 230. 3 rooms with dorm: US$6-$7. Popular with Indian families and students. No lunch served.

Hilltop Tourist Lodge (WBTDC), Tel: 654. 7 rooms: US$5-$7. Comfortable bungalow setting, large rooms, nice garden.

Deki's Lodge, 10th Mile, Tirpai Road., 8 rooms: US$3-$4 per bed. Tibetan family run, offering traditional foods and genuine hospitality. Local handicrafts displayed.

EN ROUTE TO SIKKIM-DARJEELING-KALIMPONG

Hotel Sinclairs Siliguri, P.O. Pradhan Nagar, Siliguri 734 403, West Bengal. Tel: 22674, 22675, 22440. 54 rooms: US$25-$31 (non AC/AC). With AC restaurant, clean, comfortable rooms with attached bath.

Mainak Tourist Lodge (WBTDC), Hill Cart Road, Siliguri, West Bengal, Tel: 20986, 22018, 22087. US$8-$19 (single) US$12-$25 (double). Slightly used feeling, fine for short overnight.

Seven Seas Holiday Home, Old Airport, Biratnagar, Nepal, Tel: 021-24872.

US$8-10. Best available in Biratnagar.

Hotel Mountain & Lodge, Kakarbhitta, Nepal. US$2-$3. Located north of the bus stand.

HEALTH AND EMERGENCIES

Hygiene

Drinking only boiled or bottled water. Bottled mineral waters, soft drinks and beers are safe. Eat raw vegetables and fruits only if peeled or properly treated (soaked at least 30 minutes in a potassium sterile solution). Wash your hands regularly and always before eating.

Pharmacies and Hospitals

Even with these precautions, some visitors may experience minor intestinal disorder; few require more than a bland diet and plenty of liquids. If diarrhoea persists for more than three days, get a stool test and see a doctor for treatment.

Most common medicines are available in pharmacies without a prescription and quite cheaply. In any case, it is wise to bring along your own medical kit with prescription drugs. Have a dental check-up before leaving home.

In Sikkim, there are district hospitals in Gangtok, Geyzing, Namchi and Mangan (smaller hospitals elsewhere), and in Darjeeling, Kalimpong and Siliguri (see Useful Addresses). There will generally be English speaking doctors in hospitals.

Safety and Rescue

Travel is generally quite safe, however, watch your belongings, especially in crowded places and leave valuables in a hotel safe deposit box or with your trekking agent while trekking. Women are generally unhasseled but should not walk alone late at night.

In case of an accident while in the mountains, your trekking agent can request helicopter rescue by the Indian army, but there is no guarantee that one will be available. It is best to avoid risky situations.

COMMUNICATIONS AND NEWS

Post and Telephone

The General Post Office in **Gangtok** is located on Paljor Stadium Road near the Hotel Tibet, Tel: 2385. Opening hours are 9am to 5pm. A Poste Restante desk will hold incoming mail. Packages can be shipped from here; shipping costs are posted.

Telephone, telegram and telefax counters are open from 7am to 10pm weekdays (Monday-Saturday), 8.30am to 6.30pm on government holidays and Sundays. Telefax and telegraph services are also available at the GPO. The fax receiving number is 0091-3592-2707.

The General Post Office in **Darjeeling** is located on Ladenla Road, Tel 2076. Opening hours are 10am to 6pm, Saturdays 10am to 4.30pm, Sundays closed. A Poste Restante counter receives general delivery mail.

The Telegraph Office is located on Gandhi Road, Tel: 2185. Opening hours for telephone, telegraph and telex services are 7am to 9.30pm Monday through Saturday, 8.30am to 6.30pm on Sundays and holidays.

The **Kalimpong** General Post Office, located near the Police Station, Tel: 242, is open from 10am to 6pm Monday-Friday, 10am to 3pm Saturday, closed Sundays. There is no Poste Restante service here. The Telegraph section of the same office is open Monday-Saturday 10am to 5pm, closed Sundays.

Major hotels in Gangtok, Darjeeling and Kalimpong now have direct dial international telephone service (STD), many from private room telephones. Telephone service into rural parts is limited.

Media

Indian daily newspapers and Asian weekly periodicals are available at bookshops in Gangtok, Darjeeling and Kalimpong (see Shopping). International publications can be hard to find. Nightly news is given in English on Indian television (9.30pm) and radio.

USEFUL INFORMATION

The **Sikkim Tourist Information Centre** in Gangtok is extremely helpful in planning your holiday, with English speaking staff, brochures, maps and colour posters available for a small charge. They offer sightseeing tours, excursions and can help arrange hotels, transportation, treks and rafting trips. The opening hours are 8am to 8pm during the main tourist season (March-June, September-December), otherwise according to standard office hours.

In Darjeeling, the **Tourist Bureau** on Chowrastha (at the Mall) is fully staffed to assist you with hotel reservations, transportation, sightseeing and excursions. Opening hours are 10am to 4.30pm daily except on Sundays and government holidays.

The **Darjeeling Gorkha Hill Council** (DGHC) Department of Tourism can assist with information on trekking, rafting and other adventure activities.

Kalimpong is hoping to have its own branch of the DGHC Department of Tourism soon. Contact the Tourist Bureau in Darjeeling or the West Bengal Tourism Development Corp. (WBTDC) for information, brochures and arrangements.

Language

English is widely understood throughout Sikkim, Darjeeling and Kalimpong. Some Nepalese and Sikkimese/Tibetan phrases are also helpful to know, especially when travelling in rural areas:

chaam: religious masked dances (or any dance in Sikkimese)

chiya: milk tea, usually sweetened

chorten: a small Buddhist shrine, usu-

ally with reliquary objects inside.

chu: water, or river

dhanyabaad/thuche che: thank you in Nepalese/Sikkimese

gompa: a Buddhist monastery

Kati rupiya?: How many rupees (is this)?

la: a mountain pass

lama: a Tibetan Buddhist priest

Namaste: the Nepalese greeting which means "I salute the divine spirit in you"

puja: ritual offering to the gods

Rinpoche: the abbot of a monastery

solja: Tibetan tea, prepared with butter and salt (or any tea in Sikkimese language)

Tashi Delek: the Sikkimese/Tibetan greeting offering a blessing of good fortune.

SPORTS

One day rafting trips can be arranged on the Tista River (Sikkim) during April-May and September-October. Boats put-in at Bardang and float about 8km (5 miles) down to Rangpo. Arrangements can be made at the Rangpo Tourist Lodge or with Sikkim Tourism in Gangtok, or with advertised private operators.

The cost is approximately US$12-$15 per person, including one meal (either lunch or dinner). Life-jackets and helmets are provided. Commercial rafting is now available on the Rangit River out of Darjeeling; contact the DGHC Tourism Department.

Other sports possibilities are pony rides from the Darjeeling Mall, fishing or kayaking on the Rangit or Tista, paragliding (spots yet to be designated), and boating at Darjeeling's Mirik Lake. Inquire at the Tourist Information Centres for details. Bicycles are not available for rent in any of these hill communities.

USEFUL ADDRESSES

Tourist Offices

For Sikkim:
Sikkim Tourist Information Centre, M.G. Marg, Gangtok. Tel: 2064
Department of Tourism. Tel: 3425

Sikkim Tourist Information Centre, New Sikkim House, 14 Panchsheel Marg, Chanakyapuri, New Delhi 110 021. Tel: 3015346

Sikkim Tourist Information Centre, SNT Colony, Siliguri. Tel: 24602

For Darjeeling and Kalimpong:
Tourist Bureau, Government of West Bengal, 1 Nehru Road, Darjeeling, Tel: 2050

Department of Tourism, DGHC, Tourist Bureau, Chowrastha, Darjeeling, Tel: 2524

Tourist Bureau, Government of West Bengal, Hill Cart Road, 1st Floor, Siliguri, Tel: 21632, 24650

West Bengal Tourism Development Corporation, Reservations & Information Office, 3/2 BBD Bagh East, 1st Floor, Calcutta, India 700001, Tel: 288271

Airlines

Indian Airlines
In Gangtok: Tibet Road, Tel: 3099.
In Darjeeling: The Mall, Tel: 2355
In Kalimpong: c/o Mintri Transport, Main Road, Tel: 741, 697.

Hospitals

In Sikkim: S.T.N.M. Hospital, Traffic Chowk, Tel: 2944.
In Darjeeling: D & DMA Nursing Home, Nehru Road. Tel: 3210
Sadar Hospital, near the Taxi Stand, Tel: 2218
Eden Hospital, near the Police Station, Tel: 2131
In Kalimpong: Sub-Divisional Government Hospital, Tel: 245

Police and Fire
In Sikkim: Police Station, M.G. Marg, Gangtok, Tel: 2033, 2022
In Darjeeling: Police Station, Near the Supermarket.
Fire Station: Tel: 2121
In Kalimpong: Police Station, Rinkingpong Road. Tel: 268
Fire Station: Tel: 450

FURTHER READING

Here are a few of the books specific to these eastern Himalayan communities. A plethora of books on the Himalaya cover various aspects of interest as well.

General

Bedi, Rajesh, with text by Mathur, Asharani, & Pant, Pushpesh. *Sikkim.* Bribasi Printers, New Delhi. 1989. Primarily a picture book, with Bedi's excellent coverage of all aspects of Sikkim.

Israel, Samuel and Grewal, Bikram. *Insight Guide: India.*
Apa Publications, Singapore. 1992. The usual excellent coverage of geography, culture, travel tips but with only a small section on these hill areas.

Risley, H.H. *The Gazetteer of Sikhim.* B.R. Publishing Corp. New Delhi. 1894. The best encyclopedia on Sikkim, with details on monastery particulars, religious practices, vegetation, wildlife, etc.
Sharma, Ramesh and Bedi, Rajesh. *Images of Sikkim.* Rigsum Productions. A picture account of this photogenic land.

Verma, Sunila. *A Guide to Sikkim.* Smt. Sunila Verma, Gangtok. 1990. A small tourist guide with the basics.

People, Art and Culture

Foning, A.R. *Lepcha - My Vanishing Tribe.* Sterling Publishers. 1987. An excellent personal account with insight into the life of the Lepcha people.

Kowall, Earl and Nazima. *Our World in Colour - Sikkim and Darjeeling*. The Guidebook Company Ltd. 1990. Stunning photographs with a summary text introducing Sikkim.

Politics and History

Battaglia, L.B. *Wedding of Two Worlds*. National Geographic, Vol. 124 No. 5, November 1973. Fairy-tale tinted story of the Chogyal and Hope Cooke's wedding.

Coronation Souvenir Book Committee. *Sikkim Coronation*. The Statesman Press, Calcutta. A good historical summary, description of the royal wedding and previous coronations.

Das, B.S. *The Sikkim Saga, 1973-75*. Vikas Publishing House, New Delhi. 1990. Covering the merger of Sikkim into India, and the story of three key female figures Indira Gandhi, Hope Cooke and Elisa Maria.

Field Rennie, Dr. David. *Bhotan and the Story of the Duar War*. Manjushri Publishing House. 1970. A well researched account of the Bhutanese wars as they effected Kalimpong.

Natural History and Trekking

Ali, Salim. *The Birds of Sikkim*. Oxford University Press, New Delhi. 1989. Describing over 400 bird species of Sikkim, with 140 colour illustrations and 36 black and white sketches.

Pradhan, Udai C. and Lachungpa, Sonam T.. *Sikkim-Himalayan Rhododendrons*. Primulaceae Books, Kalimpong, India. 1990. A compendium of Himalayan Rhododendrons with hand-painted plates of 40 species — a collector's item.

Swift, Hugh. *Trekking in Pakistan and India*. Sierra Club Books. San Francisco. 1990. One of the only trekking books covering Sikkim, in the usual entertaining, practical Swift style.

Acknowledgements

This book was accomplished with the much appreciated assistance and expertise of the following people:

Menuka Bhattacharjee, Darjeeling
K.K. Bhutia, New Delhi
Mr and Mrs Pempo Thondup Bhutia, Temi, Sikkim
Karma Sonam Bhutia, Gangtok, Sikkim
Lisa Choegyal, Kathmandu, Nepal
Jamyang Dorje, Gangtok, Sikkim
Karma Gyatso, Gangtok, Sikkim
Karma Lama, Kathmandu, Nepal
Arthur Pazo, Kathmandu, Nepal
Udai and Tej Pradhan, Kalimpong
Mr and Mrs R.K. Spring, Kalimpong
Amode Yonzone, Kalimpong

Art & Photo Credits

Photography by and 16T, 21, 24, 25T&B, 30, 31, 36T, 40, 41T&B, 43T&B, 47T, 48, 53, 55B, 56T&B, 62B, 69, 71, 73, 75T&B, 76 **Wendy Brewer Lama**

11T, 14T, 15, 16B, 27, 35, 36B, 42, 46, 47B, 55T, 61, 62T, 63, 65, 80, 82, 86, 89T, 92 **Sujoy Das**

11B, 12, 13T&B, 14B, 28, 32B, 59, 64, 67, 77, 78, 90B **Arthur Pazo**

1, 4, 18T, 29T&B, 33, 34, 52, 54, 57, 66, 72, 84, 85 **Gary McCue**

10, 20, 44, 45 **A. V. Lockwood**

32T, 37, 68, 89M, 90M **Amit Ray**

19 **Ashvin Mehta**

Sikkim

16 km / 10 miles